December 2 1986

To my brother Jack —

With very warmest

*B*c

PACIFIC RIM
Area of Change,
Area of Opportunity

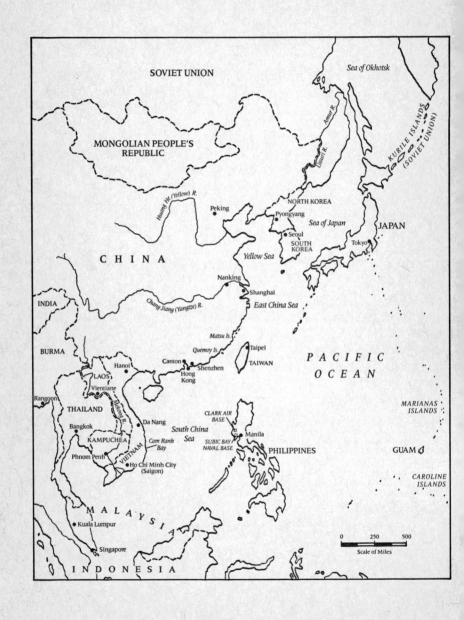

PACIFIC RIM
Area of Change,
Area of Opportunity

David Aikman

LITTLE, BROWN AND COMPANY
BOSTON,   TORONTO

FIRST EDITION

Library of Congress Cataloging-in-Publication Data

Aikman, David, 1944–

Pacific Rim : area of change, area of opportunity.

1. East Asia — Politics and government. 2. East Asia —
Economic conditions.   3. Asia, Southeastern — Politics
and government.   4. Asia, Southeastern — Economic
conditions.   I. Title.
DS518.1.A525   1986   959   86-2802
ISBN 0-316-02039-7

RRD VA

Designed by Robert G. Lowe

Published simultaneously in Canada
by Little, Brown & Company (Canada) Limited

PRINTED IN THE UNITED STATES OF AMERICA

For Nonie, and for Abigail and Amanda

CONTENTS

ACKNOWLEDGMENTS

THIS BOOK could not have come into existence without the support, involvement, and generous cooperation of several people.

I am, first of all, indebted to the editors and corporate officers of *Time* magazine for encouraging me to go ahead with the project and giving me time away from my normal reporting duties to do so. I am particularly grateful to Editor-in-Chief of Time Incorporated Henry Anatole Grunwald and Assistant Managing Editor for Administration (also formerly Chief of Correspondents) Richard L. Duncan in this respect. I would like to thank John A. Meyers, then Publisher of *Time* magazine, now Chairman of Time Inc.'s Magazine Group, for inviting me to participate in the Time Newstour '85: Pacific Rim, and for backing the publication of a book on the Pacific Rim theme from the outset. I also owe a debt of gratitude to Reginald K. Brack, Jr., Group Vice-President, Publishing, and to Ray C. Cave, Corporate Editor of Time Inc., for their wise counsel. Robert D. Sweeney, Worldwide Public Affairs Director for *Time* magazine, generously secured a research assistant for me.

My gratitude to Little, Brown and Company is immense. My editor, Fredrica S. Friedman, deserves a particular bouquet from me for her clarity of vision, wise judgment, and patience.

My researcher, Carrie Welch, was intelligent, calm, and inde-
fatigable in eliciting sometimes obscure information at very short
notice. I could not have asked for a better assistant.

Robert Gottlieb, Vice-President of the William Morris Agency
and my literary agent, was as gracious, efficient, and supportive
as ever in overseeing the arrangements with my publisher. He
deserves my profound thanks.

Several *Time* magazine colleagues contributed more than they
may realize to the book with their insights, knowledge, and experience in the Pacific Rim. Fellow correspondents Sandra Burton
and Bing W. Wong in Hong Kong, Benjamin W. Cate on the
Newstour, Edwin M. Reingold and S. Chang in Tokyo, Richard
Hornik in Peking, and James Willwerth in Bangkok were all outstanding in this respect. Friendship with them over the years has
been a pleasure and a privilege.

Finally, and with considerable pleasure, I would like to thank
the participants in Time Newstour '85 for their role in illuminating
for me so many of the key issues of the Pacific Rim. Space does
not permit me to name here the many who freely shared with me
their thoughts on the Pacific Rim and numerous related topics
during the Newstour in October–November 1985. In many ways
their individual excellence as leaders of the U.S. corporate and
civic community was an inspiration for this book.

All this said, it only needs to be added that no one other than
I should bear responsibility for whatever shortcomings there are
in these pages.

PREFACE

THE GROWING IMPORTANCE of the Pacific has been obvious to many astute observers of international relations over the past few years. It has given rise to numerous international and trans-pacific gatherings of academics, business people, and professionals eager to understand the phenomenon and, if possible, influence it benignly. A small number of books have appeared, summing up such gatherings and groping toward a consensus of views about the issues facing the people and lands rimming the Pacific. In addition, several books over the years, many of them excellent, have delved into the specific countries of the Pacific Rim or into separate, regional issues particular to the area.

Perhaps because the Pacific itself is so vast and so diverse as a political or economic theme, surprisingly few books have attempted to sum up the principal issues of the region for the general reader or to outline the key implications of developments in it for Americans. This book is, in that respect, an effort to fill what is probably a serious gap. It does not attempt to deal systematically with each of the fourteen or so countries generally recognized as belonging to the Pacific Rim, much less to discuss in encyclopedic manner those countries which are examined at some length in it. Even less does it claim to be the last word on East Asia as a whole or on U.S. diplomatic and economic policy for the region. But it does attempt to introduce to the general reader, and especially to American business leaders, the most important recent and likely future issues of the Pacific Rim as a geographic and economic entity.

Many books have precipitating events behind them, and *Pacific Rim: Area of Change, Area of Opportunity* is one of these. It grew out of an unusual, seventeen-day trip to seven Pacific Rim countries taken by a group of thirty-three senior U.S. executives and prominent public figures during late October and early November 1985, and organized by *Time* magazine. The trip was called "Time Newstour '85: Pacific Rim." Some twenty-one executives, editors, and correspondents from *Time*'s parent company, Time Incorporated, also participated in the Newstour.

The term "Newstour" is probably unfamiliar to most readers and thus needs a brief explanation. In 1963, *Time* organized the first such tour, a visit to the Soviet Union and Eastern Europe by a delegation of senior *Time* executives, editors, and correspondents, and several invited prominent American business leaders. Since then, including Newstour '85, there have been eight Newstours. Each has ranged in duration from one to two and a half weeks and has focused on a selected area of the world: Southeast Asia, Eastern Europe, and the Far East in the 1960s, for example; the Middle East, and South Africa in the 1970s; Eastern Europe, the Middle East, and Mexico in the 1980s.

Neither business trips nor vacation outings, Newstours have resembled most closely the itinerary that a managing editor of a major American news organization might be expected to draw up for a rapid fact-finding visit to an important part of the world. Organized by *Time* staffers, Time Newstours are heavily scheduled journalistic forays into a given region of the world for executives interested in the area.

The Pacific Rim Newstour, which set out from San Francisco on October 18, 1985, was both typical of previous Newstour formats, and in some ways more ambitious than they were. Over the course of seventeen days it visited six countries and one city-state:

South Korea, China, Hong Kong, Taiwan, the Philippines, Vietnam, Thailand. It also included a longer single-country stay — four days in China — than any previous tour had. The Time Newstour '85 was conceived entirely as a private visit, representing neither the U.S. government nor any particular editorial position of *Time* or Time Inc. Since the Newstour's participants represented corporations with collective sales figures amounting to nearly a quarter of the U.S. GNP, however, the group attracted considerable attention at most stops along the itinerary. The Newstour also generated a small but intriguing footnote to the history of U.S.–Southeast Asian relations.

The incident arose when the Department of State in Washington learned that the Newstour, flying in a chartered TWA 747 jet, would be landing directly in Hanoi. At a time when the United States itself had no diplomatic relations with Vietnam, some Washington officials worried that Hanoi might not fully grasp the entirely unofficial nature of the Newstour. Vietnamese officials, the Department of State told Newstour participants before their departure, might reach the mistaken conclusion that Washington was better disposed to Vietnam than had previously been indicated.

These fears were not borne out by events, as the State Department later acknowledged privately to *Time* and to Newstour participants. The Newstour was indeed seen by Hanoi as a major event in its own right, since it turned out to be the largest U.S. delegation to visit the country since the end of the war. But during interviews with Premier Pham Van Dong, published in *Time*, and with other Vietnamese officials, the visiting Americans reaffirmed the fact-finding, rather than commercial or diplomatic, essence of their trip, and the Vietnamese made no further attempt to represent the Newstour as anything other than a privately sponsored enterprise.

Time staffers provided extensive preparatory material for the Newstour participants several weeks before the group left San Francisco, gave briefings both before the departure and at various points along the trip, and made the arrangements for meetings with government and opposition leaders in all of the countries visited. In addition, there were two specific meetings during the tour where the participants were invited to reflect aloud on their impressions up to that point. The first, an informal one, was in Shanghai, appropriately enough in the guest house where Chairman Mao had stayed during his periodic absences from Peking in the 1960s and 1970s. The second was a formal concluding session in Bangkok at which all thirty-three of the invited participants were asked to sum up their insights and reflections. At no point during the Newstour was there any attempt either by *Time* editors and staffers or by the invited participants to extrapolate a consensus of views on what they had seen and heard or on regional issues as a whole.

What the Newstour provided was a unique exposure within a very short space of time to the heart of some of the most important issues facing East Asia and the world as a whole. A sense of the region's pulse emerged from it, along with a feeling for the diverse and often colorful personalities of the Pacific Rim's leaders. In addition, an important dimension of understanding was provided by the comments and reactions to present-day East Asia of a sophisticated and significant representative portion of the U.S. business community. As had been the case in previous Newstours organized by *Time*, many of the most interesting insights of the participants occurred during chance conversations at different points of the itinerary.

Much of the material for this book came from the intense and vivid encounters with key countries of the Pacific Rim during the Time Newstour '85. Some of the ideas in it were inspired by, or at least coincided with, views expressed by the Newstour participants, either during the Bangkok wrap-up discussion, or more informally during the trip itself.

It should nevertheless be stressed that this book in no way claims to represent the views, either individually or collectively, of *Time* editors or of Newstour participants. The assessment it contains is purely a personal one. *Pacific Rim: Area of Change, Area of Opportunity* is an introduction to some of the key issues of East Asia and an investigation of the region at a very concrete and very recent point in its history.

* * *

The following persons were *Time's* invited participants in the Time Newstour '85: Pacific Rim:

Robert Anderson, Chairman of Rockwell International Corporation; Dwayne O. Andreas, Chairman of Archer Daniels Midland Company; Warren L. Batts, President of Dart & Kraft, Inc.; Drummond C. Bell, Chairman of National Distillers and Chemical Corporation; Walter R. F. Bodack, President of Mercedes-Benz of North America; Edgar Bronfman, Jr., President of The House of Seagram; Theodore F. Brophy, Chairman of GTE Corporation; Donald W. Davis, Chairman of The Stanley Works; John F. Doyle, Chairman of Pioneer Electronics (USA) Inc.; Myron du Bain, Member of the Board of Directors and former President of Amfac Inc.; Henry C. Goodrich, former Chairman of Sonat Inc.; Donald E. Guinn, Chairman of Pacific Telesis Group; James R. Harvey, Chairman and President of Transamerica Corporation; Alexander Heard, Chancellor Emeritus of Vanderbilt University; Carla Anderson Hills, Managing Partner of Latham, Watkins & Hills; Matina S. Horner, President of Radcliffe College; John E. Jacob, President of the National Urban League; T. Lawrence Jones, President of the American Insurance Association; Sol M. Linowitz, Senior Counsel of Coudert Brothers; Henry Luce III, President of the Henry Luce Foundation Inc.; Robert H. Malott, Chairman of FMC Corporation; Donald F. McHenry, University Research Professor of Diplomacy and International Relations at Georgetown University; Robert E. Mercer, Chairman of the Goodyear Tire & Rubber Company; John A. Murphy, President of Philip Morris Companies Inc.; John J. Nevin, Chairman and President of the Firestone Tire & Rubber Company; Charles W. Parry, Chairman of the Aluminum Company of America; Donald S. Perkins, former Chairman of Jewel Companies Inc.; Forrest N. Shumway, Chairman of The Signal Companies, Inc.; Robert J. Sinclair, President of Saab-Scania of America, Inc.; John G. Smale, President of the Proctor & Gamble Company; Preston Robert Tisch, President of the Loews Corporation; William A. Walker, President of Bacardi Imports, Inc.; Clifton R. Wharton, Jr., Chancellor of the State University of New York and Chairman of the Rockefeller Foundation.

PACIFIC RIM
Area of Change,
Area of Opportunity

1

THE PACIFIC RIM
The Challenge

"WESTERN HISTORY BEGAN with a Mediterranean era, passed through an Atlantic era, and is now moving into a Pacific era." Ever since President Theodore Roosevelt's Secretary of State John Hay uttered these words in 1902, their prophetic truth has become more and more vivid in the fabric of American life. Today, the "Pacific era" is already well upon us. Whether we like it or not, the destiny of the United States is being inextricably linked to developments taking place around the edge of the Pacific Ocean: around the Pacific Rim, to use the phrase that has increasingly become the standard way of referring to the region.

The term "Pacific Rim" itself derives from physical geography. It refers to the rim of active volcanoes around the edge of the Pacific, including not only the well-known volcanic zone that passes through Japan and the Philippines, but also the long volcanic and earthquake-prone ribbon that runs from the northern Pacific down the West Coast of the United States and beyond to South America, known as the San Andreas Fault. In theory, therefore, the term as we and others use it should also refer to the Pacific countries of North, Central, and South America. In practice, it has come to denote something rather different: the significant trading countries of the Asian section of the Pacific, together with the United States and Canada, these nations' principal trading partners. Sometimes these East Asian and Australasian countries are also referred to by the phrase "Pacific Basin." That term is, of course, entirely valid in its own right. It nevertheless seems to imply a far larger geographical sweep of countries than does "Pacific Rim," including all of the newly independent island archipelagic nations of the central and south Pacific.

This book focuses on the countries of the East Asian edge of the Pacific and their impact upon the United States. For this reason, along with the tendency of increasing numbers of international conferences to use the term "Pacific Rim" to designate both the geographical area and a loosely joined economic and political community, we have preferred that term.

Informally, the phrase tends to be specifically applied to the following fifteen important trading countries (in the case of Hong Kong, of course, "country" is shorthand: it remains a colony of Great Britain until 1997, when it reverts fully to China): the United States, Canada, Japan, Korea, China, Hong Kong, Taiwan, the Philippines, Thailand, Malaysia, Singapore, Indonesia, Brunei, Australia, and New Zealand. Most of the time, this book will use the term "Pacific Rim" to denote the major East Asian members of the community — South Korea, Japan, Hong Kong, Taiwan, the Philippines, Thailand — in order to distinguish them from the United States and Canada. When the emerging community of the "Pacific Rim" as a whole is being discussed, this will be clear from the context.

"Rim" or "Basin," or simply "East Asia," the Pacific challenge has nevertheless emphatically arrived on America's doorstep and is growing increasingly impatient to be addressed. The challenge is multifaceted: economic, political, strategic, even philosophical. At stake is the future peaceful and economically successful development of some 60 percent of the population of the world and the successful participation by American business in one of the most dynamic potential market areas of all time. Also at stake is American resolve in facing up to — and if necessary, facing down — a conspicuously growing effort by the Soviet Union to expand its strategic and political influence in the Pacific Ocean. America's sense of "Manifest Destiny" in the Pacific became strongly evident in the nineteenth century. That of the Soviet Union has barely begun.

The areas of risk in the Pacific challenge are many and obvious and will emerge clearly enough, we hope, in these pages. But, as with the glass of water that is either half-full or half-empty according to the perspective of the viewer, they should not eclipse the broad and exciting vistas of opportunities for the United States in the region — mainly, the unprecedented opportunities for American business exports. Short of a global economic collapse, commerce in the Pacific Rim will continue to grow at enormous speed. The United States can and must be part of it. Whether the field is computers, advanced aerospace, communications breakthroughs, or perhaps some hitherto unforeseen agriculturally based product, Americans are being challenged by the emergence of a world trading zone that has grown at an unprecedented rate and shows no evidence of even approaching its limits. By the year 2000 almost two-thirds of the world's consumers will be living around the edge of the Pacific. By that year, too, trade with this area is expected to constitute more than 25 percent of the American GNP. (In 1959, it was only 6 percent. Today, it is 17 percent.)

The natural resources of the Pacific Rim are considerable, especially those in Thailand, Malaysia, and Indonesia. But, if anything, it is the human resources, the cultural richness and its adaptability to modern commerce, that are the most exciting aspects of the region. The close family ties, sense of social discipline, and deep respect for hard work are outstanding features of those Pacific Rim societies influenced by China's traditional philosophy of Confucianism. South Korea, Japan, Hong Kong, and Singapore have shown in a dramatic way how "traditional" Asian cultural norms have eased the adaptation of backward economies to the fast-moving economies of the advanced industrial world. Though for a while the United States itself appeared to be questioning, in the 1960s and 1970s, the value of the Protestant work ethic, the societies of the Pacific Rim during the same period were growing more and more prosperous by zealously practicing their own ver-

sion of the same thing. Perhaps "Confucian work ethic," or a
similar term, should be used to describe the phenomenon of un-
coerced hard work and sacrifice by millions of Pacific Rim families
that has characterized the area's post–World War II development.

These human resources have made possible an exponential increase in Pacific trade. They have also opened up the possibilities
of mutual, transpacific intellectual, social, cultural, and political
stimulus, in a beneficial way, for the Pacific Rim community as a
whole. American society itself has already been invigorated by the
energies brought into it over a handful of decades by talented Asian-
Americans in many areas of endeavor. The Pacific Rim, similarly,
has continued to ferment with American political and social ideas,
even as the community's economy has prospered under the stimulus of manifestly American ideas of free market economics. Both
North America and the East Asian segment of the Pacific Rim are
likely to be stimulated in further ways, difficult even to imagine at
present, as the interflow of contacts and ideas grows in momentum.

Already, an awareness of the growing commonality of Pacific
Rim interests has spawned a variety of international, nongovern-
mental, transpacific groups: the Pacific Science Association, the
Pacific Forum, the Pacific Basin Economic Council, and the Pacific
Economic Cooperation Conference, to name but a few. No doubt
many others will follow. The world, after all, is still absorbing the
colossal dynamic of intercultural and political creativity set in motion during the Mediterranean era of early historical times. It is
certainly not fanciful to predict at least as far-reaching an impact
upon mankind from the ferment produced by a new "Pacific era"
coming into being now and developing in the next century.

In the spirit of his predecessor John Hay, President Reagan's
Secretary of State George Shultz has spoken eloquently and often
of this new Pacific era. Addressing in February 1985 the U.S.
National Committee for Pacific Economic Cooperation, Shultz
claimed that in the Pacific today, there was now "a new reality,
though the world may not yet fully comprehend it. In economic
development," he added, "in the growth of free institutions, and
in growing global influence, the Pacific region has rapidly emerged

as a leading force on the world stage. . . . A sense of Pacific community is emerging."

Shultz, a Republican, was not repeating any politically partisan dictum. Less than a year later, prominent Democratic Senator Gary Hart of Colorado used almost identical words at another conference on the Pacific Rim in Laguna Niguel, California, in December 1985. "We are all," he said, "members of the community of nations surrounding the Pacific." If anything, Hart waxed even more eloquent about the Pacific than had John Hay or George Shultz. "The Pacific has become," he declared, "the twentieth century's economic fountain of youth."

A fountain indeed. The statistics of the Pacific Rim's emergence into the front ranks of global economic power are imposing. In the course of barely a quarter of a century several Asian countries have emerged as global trading powers of the first magnitude. Averaging annual economic growth rates approaching 10 percent in some cases, the Pacific Rim countries of Japan, South Korea, Taiwan, Thailand, Singapore, and Hong Kong have collectively surpassed every other region in the world in economic performance. The engine of their growth was world trade, and much of the fuel for it was the gigantic domestic market of the United States.

A notion of what has happened is best provided by a comparison of the Pacific Rim's world trade position with that of Western Europe. Throughout most of U.S. history, including the several decades during which America has possessed the largest national economy in the world, its principal world trading partners were the countries of Western Europe. Since 1980, all that has changed. In that year, for the first time ever, U.S. trade with Asia surpassed that with Western Europe, 28 percent to 22 percent. Europe, of course, still occupied a much bigger slice of total world trade than did the Pacific Rim countries: in 1982, the figure was 32 percent to 15 percent. But Pacific Rim trade has been growing at a much faster rate than Western European trade. By the year 2000, it may well have completely caught up with Western European trade volume, with each region taking up 20 percent of the global total.

Profile of Pacific Rim Countries Compared with the United States for the Year 1985

	South Korea	China	Hong Kong	Taiwan	Philippines	Vietnam	Thailand	United States
AREA	38,259 sq. mi.	3,695,500 sq. mi.	412 sq. mi.	13,900 sq. mi.	115,831 sq. mi.	127,246 sq. mi.	198,115 sq. mi.	3,617,733 sq. mi.
POPULATION (1985 est.)	42.7 million	1,046 million	5.5 million	19.2 million	56.8 million	60.5 million	52.7 million	238.7 million
DENSITY	1,116/sq. mi.	282/sq. mi.	13,349/sq. mi.	1,381/sq. mi.	490/sq. mi.	475/sq. mi.	266/sq. mi.	66/sq. mi.
GNP (1985)	$83.1 billion	$264.9 billion*	$33.27 billion*	$60.1 billion	$29.13 billion	$7.9 billion	$37.2 billion	$4,059 billion
GNP per capita (1985)	$2,032	$253	$6,090†	$3,147	$533	$130	$725	$16,150
ADULT LITERACY	94.3%	77%	75%	89.7%	88%	78%	84%	99.5%
INFANT MORTALITY	29/1,000	38/1,000	9.9/1,000	8.9/1,000	50/1,000	90/1,000	51/1,000	10.5/1,000
EXPORTS (F.O.B. 1985)	$30.27 billion	$26.5 billion	$30.18 billion	$30.7 billion	$4.63 billion	$600 million	$7.1 billion	$213.15 billion
BALANCE OF TRADE	–$882 million	–$13.7 billion	$0.48 billion	$10. 5 billion	–$1 billion	–$1.1 billion	–$2.2 billion	–$148.5 billion

*Gross Domestic Product
†Gross Domestic Product per capita

The American role in this growth has been seminal. From the late 1970s, East Asian trade with the United States has increased two and a half times the rate of U.S. trade with the rest of the world, 25 percent to 10 percent. Each year, the dollar volume amounts to some $30 billion more than the total of U.S. trade with Western Europe. In 1984, four out of ten of the United States's top trading partners were Pacific Rim countries: Japan, South Korea, Taiwan, and Hong Kong. By 1983, South Korea's trade with the United States had already overtaken that of such formidable economic powers, in global terms, as France, Italy, and the Netherlands. South Korea itself, along with Taiwan and Hong Kong, already belonged to the four "NICs," an acronym coined by dazzled economists for Newly Industrialized Country, and referring to South Korea, Taiwan, Hong Kong, and Singapore. The NICs, in world trade terms, had on their own carved out a great chunk of total world commerce. With a combined population of only 70 million, the total of their trade with the United States in 1984 exceeded the entire $57 billion of U.S. trade with all of South America and the Middle East combined. Only when Mexico's oil-based exports of $30 billion are added to the Latin American–Middle East total do the scales finally tip against the NICs.

The Pacific Rim's NICs did well by Asian standards. By comparison with the majority of developing countries, though, their economic growth jumped off the graph. In 1984, they accounted for 70 percent of the entire world trade of the more than 100 developing countries. Yet they took up less than 20 percent of the developing world's total debt, and collectively had some of the best debt service ratios, the percentage of export earnings needed to pay the interest on outstanding loans. A principal NIC trading partner, Japan, a highly industrialized, advanced Pacific Rim country, meanwhile averaged a growth rate of 5.9 percent between 1960 and 1984, achieving what could arguably be considered one of the most remarkable sustained economic performances of a major country at any time in history. During this period, the Japanese economy was growing at a rate two-thirds faster than that of the United States and twice that of France and West Germany, the fastest-growing countries in Western Europe.

Trade, trade, and more trade was what propelled the Pacific Rim states out of agrarian destitution or post–World War II destruction and decline into world economic prominence. Generously, and in consonance with its own economic and philosophical principles, the United States opened itself up to import the goods manufactured by the Pacific Rim states. The current prosperity of the Pacific Rim countries is a direct consequence of the openness of the U.S. domestic market, especially in the area of consumer desires. This commercially hospitable environment has enabled countries or trading partners such as Japan, South Korea, Hong Kong, Taiwan, and Singapore to bring an unmatched prosperity to their own people, thus providing a firm economic base for internal political stability. In a speech to a joint session of the U.S. Congress in October 1985, Singapore's Prime Minister Lee Kuan Yew put it succinctly: "The United States," he said, "was the dynamo which hastened economic developments."

Regrettably, these same "developments" have been a major factor in the alarming growth of the United States's own colossal trade deficit. More than 50 percent of the United States's current trade deficit of nearly $150 billion is with Pacific Rim countries, and the proportion is growing. The U.S. deficit with Japan alone was a gigantic $39.5 billion in 1985, out of a total two-way trade of $91.4 billion. Only the $112 billion trade with Canada was higher overall. In Japan's case, moreover, there was little likelihood of any decrease in its trade surplus with the United States in the near future. Even the decline in value of the dollar early in 1986, which had the effect of pushing up import prices, had little impact upon Japanese sales in the U.S. market. Initial 1986 Japanese car sales in the United States showed that even price increases of a few hundred dollars could hardly dent American demand for the imported products of proven quality produced in the Pacific Rim.

The impact of this Pacific Rim trade imbalance with the United States has had some unavoidable negative consequences. Approximately 2 million American jobs may have been lost because of it.

The figure is likely to rise if the U.S.–Pacific Rim trade deficit further increases significantly. With it may come growing demands for protectionist measures in the U.S. Congress, demands that few congressmen will be bold enough to oppose indefinitely if the relationship between increasing imports and a decline in the U.S. job market in key manufacturing areas is further demonstrated.

Senator Hart put the challenge rather starkly at the Laguna Niguel conference already mentioned. "In 1985," he said, "the Pacific region is proclaimed an economic miracle. But what will be said in the year 2000? Not all the possibilities are attractive." The Pacific Rim, he suggested, could conceivably embark on what he called "decades of peace" if events developed happily for the region. If not, he warned, it could well drift inexorably into trade protectionism, resurgent nationalism, and economic stagnation.

Hart is certainly not alone in his forebodings about the Pacific Rim if the challenge of the U.S. Pacific trade deficit is not met wisely. Some 300 protectionist trade bills, ranging from modest proposals to firebrand decrees, have been set before the Congress. Agitation for their passage continues among some American businesses that have suffered from the Pacific Rim competition, and among labor unions understandably worried about the seemingly threatened livelihood of their members.

Yet among specialists in world trade there is almost universal agreement that the satisfaction of protectionist clamor in the United States would have far-reaching and serious consequences for the entire political and economic stability of the Pacific Rim. At the same time, many observers feel, protectionism itself would do little in the medium or long term to improve the ratio of U.S. exports, the crux of the trade deficit issue. New protectionist measures could undo all of the patient efforts — some already successful, others likely to become so — by U.S. diplomats and trade representatives to break down existing restrictive practices in the Pacific Rim countries. Worse, they would invite a series of new protectionist moves in retaliation. These, in turn, would elicit countermoves, summoning up a vicious cycle of import restrictions throughout the region, and ultimately throughout the world. The consequences of such a train of events for both the United States and the Pacific Rim community would be very serious.

Paradoxically, it is in thinking through the risky downside of the Pacific Rim trade explosion that one comprehends precisely what a tremendous impact for good in East Asia that development itself has had — more even than the U.S. defense umbrella that has protected the Pacific Rim countries from Communist external assault since the 1950s. Political stability in the region has grown on the back of rising living standards and widespread expectations of even better days. Economic growth has in most of the Pacific Rim countries reduced poverty to small, clearly identifiable islands in an archipelago of prosperity, amid a larger sea of sufficiency. It has also taken the edge off income disparity, even in some cases reducing it, and elsewhere strengthening the conviction that state redistribution of wealth at the bottom of society is less beneficial to most people most of the time than is fostering the creation of wealth by some for the benefit of all. The peoples of the Pacific Rim countries, many of whose economic leaders have absorbed the principles of capitalist economics after studying them in the United States itself, have come to discover many of their benefits firsthand. Yet the effects of the serious recession likely to follow a trade war could be socially and politically explosive, fueling demands for radical, and even totalitarian, political solutions in the more politically fragile countries of the region.

This would be especially tragic in light of one of the world's most promising political developments of the past three decades. Though none of the East Asian Pacific Rim countries, including even Japan, yet enjoys the measure of political, economic, and social freedoms available in the United States, all of them enjoy levels of civil liberty today that were not attainable in the past, and still simply do not exist in most of the developing world. There is a substantially free press and a trend toward even greater press freedom throughout the region. Society as a whole is largely free of state interference in all nonpolitical domains of activity, including education and religion. Many of the government, business, and academic leaders of Pacific Rim countries were educated in the United States and have brought back to their own societies visions of economic, social, cultural, and ultimately political freedom bound to influence others among their countries' emerging leaders in this direction. As a clear illustration of this trend, the strongly authoritarian countries of Taiwan and South Korea both have been willing to inch toward real political democracy as domestic prosperity has increased and the principles of market competition have begun to spill over from the economic arena to the political one. No one could say that this progress has been smooth, least of all those still in political opposition. But the fact is, it has taken place. That it has done so must be credited to the easing of social pressures through a constant increase in prosperity, which in turn grew out of the benevolent trade developments of the past few decades.

The dangers that could arise from Pacific Rim misunderstandings over trade are, of course, certainly not the only challenge Americans must face as they head into the Pacific century. While the United States has launched forth boldly in its encounters with East Asia, the Soviet Union has sought vigorously to carve out its own Pacific destiny and to prevent, if it can, the evolution of Pacific Rim nations increasingly away from one-party, centralized states, into pluralistic, open societies capable of sustained, peaceful, and fundamentally stable internal evolution. This second, strategic challenge has, so to speak, crept up on the United States in the very wake of the American success story in the Pacific community. It is useful to put this development into historical perspective.

In 1903, President Theodore Roosevelt confidently asserted that the United States's position in the Pacific was "such as to insure [the United States's] peaceful domination of its waters." That is certainly not true today. For much of the post–World War II period, ships of the U.S. Seventh Fleet, headquartered in Hawaii, did indeed maintain something of a benevolent Pax Americana over the entire Pacific. In the past half decade, however, the American position has been steadily, but worryingly, challenged by the Pacific fleet of the Soviet Union, based in Vladivostok. Though it still lacks the extent of warm-water port facilities that are available to the United States in much of the Pacific, the Soviet Union's Pacific fleet is larger than its two other blue-water fleets, the Black Sea and the Atlantic fleets, with 441 surface ships and 134 submarines. If it chose to do so, the Soviet Pacific fleet could play havoc with the sea-lanes that are the life-blood of Pacific Rim trade.

It is still not entirely clear what the Soviet Union is "choosing" to do in East Asia. Its increasingly visible presence within the Pacific Rim community, though, is likely to have at the very least a sub-liminal political impact upon the nations of the region. The Soviet navy today operates out of the fine harbor American engineers built at Cam Ranh Bay in southern Vietnam, and Soviet long-range Tupolev-95 Bear reconnaissance aircraft patrol the length and breadth of the South and East China seas. What has made the acquisition of Cam Ranh Bay particularly valuable for Moscow is that it is the first major warm-water port open to the Soviet fleet in the Pacific. If hostilities between the Soviet Union and the West should break out in the Pacific Rim region, the Soviet Pacific fleet could prove a serious menace to shipping in the Sea of Japan or the South China Sea. Every country in the Pacific Rim community would be dramatically affected in that event, though none more so than Japan, whose entire economic survival depends on its — or its allies' — ability to keep the sea-lanes open.

Fortunately, a beneficial countertendency to the growth of So-viet power in the Pacific Rim has been the emergence of China as a real regional peacekeeper. Though the People's Republic is not a member of the intimate, non-Communist trading group within the larger Pacific Rim community, its evolution from belligerent exporter of revolution to eager manufacturer of Cabbage Patch Kids under the Deng Xiaoping reform regime has been a vital element in building up regional confidence in the Pacific Rim. Peking has preserved the balance of power in Indochina, not only by serving as an intermediary among the different anti-Vietnamese Khmer factions, but also by directly supplying arms and other support to them through Thailand. The Chinese interest, obviously, is to keep the Hanoi regime as extended as possible, and in general to wear it down. In addition, China has played a behind-the-scenes, but important, role in cooling down the aggressive tendencies of North Korea.

China naturally has its own agenda for political and diplomatic advancement in the world community. It would be naive, moreover, to assume that Peking's de facto alignment with the Pacific Rim community against the Soviet Union will remain unchanged for the indefinite future. China's priorities in relation to Taiwan, for example, do not coincide with the United States's, as they do in Indochina. Until this issue is resolved, there will be potential for instability in the Peking-Taipei relationship. There are also risks in the new relationship that Hong Kong has acquired with China, pending the full resumption of Chinese control and sovereignty in 1997. Overall, though, however uncertain the future, the present political orientation of China is truly beneficial to the Pacific Rim community.

China's mature diplomacy certainly helps temper other challenges that lurk in the region: the nationalist megalomania and xenophobia of North Korea under Kim Il-sung, the dangers of a spillover into Thailand of Vietnamese aggression in Kampuchea, and any sudden turn for the worse in the Philippines under President Corazon Aquino. However unlikely it may now have become in the wake of the ouster of President Ferdinand Marcos, the fall of the Philippines to Communism would be a body blow to the integrity of a key grouping of the Pacific Rim, the ASEAN (Association of Southeast Asian Nations) countries of the Philippines, Thailand, Malaysia, Singapore, Indonesia, and Brunei.

Ultimately, these security challenges to the Pacific Rim community must be addressed on the American side primarily by U.S. experts and officials concerned with diplomacy and military strategy. In some areas Washington may be able to have a significant impact upon events — by maintaining a high profile in South Korea, for example, or by backing up with financial aid its public commitment to the regime of President Aquino — but in other areas there may be little the United States can do to affect developments.

What is vital is that Americans should keep a clear perspective on the interrelationships within the region, and not attempt to build policy piecemeal and on a country-by-country basis.

To this end, the United States can be truly influential also in providing the framework for Pacific Rim self-awareness as a community. The U.S. National Committee for Pacific Economic Cooperation, inaugurated in the White House in September 1984, sends a signal to the area that Washington strongly supports exploratory interregional discussion on greater Pacific Rim cooperation. Because the committee is politically bipartisan, it also reaffirms what must be a fundamental principle of American involvement in the Pacific: that U.S. commitment to the region goes beyond differences of policies over the means to meet that commitment.

Firm political determination will be needed in Washington to maintain this commitment, and a courageous refusal among U.S. legislators not to be swept away by demands from their constituents for short-term palliatives to the U.S. foreign trade deficit.

American business, labor, and academic community leaders thus have the responsibility to play a major role in identifying for the American population as a whole the Pacific Rim as an area of opportunity rather than of threat. The adoption of a forward-looking strategy will influence the constituencies in which they are respected and will steady the current and subsequent U.S. administrations as they confront new and inevitably challenging tests of American ingenuity and resolve in the region. Time and again it has been clear expressions of will from the American public that have provided the occasionally fickle Executive Branch with the muscle needed to grasp and overcome nettlesome problems. In Manila, Washington moved decisively to ease Marcos out of power at a time when pusillanimity might have tempted the aging bureaucrat to miscalculate on his chances of political survival. That, in turn, could have led to a bloodbath. But a clear American national consensus buttressed the arguments of those within the State Department and the White House who favored sending an unequivocal message of nonsupport to Marcos.

Farsighted U.S. companies will meanwhile no doubt be mapping out their strategies for moving decisively into Pacific Rim markets not just for the next few years, but for the next few decades. The Pacific Rim's challenge to American business is as novel as the opportunities that come with it. Americans unused to or uninterested in learning the intricacies of foreign languages and cultures may find themselves compelled by foreign competition to change their attitudes. High technology no doubt will sell itself in the Pacific Rim market as well as anywhere: a Boeing 747 is an excellent aircraft regardless of the language of the pilot. But many Pacific markets into which U.S. companies, big and small, will be heading will demand more of the intellectual and cultural resources of Americans than has ever been the case in the great American pursuit of commerce around the world.

There is every likelihood American executives and diplomats will display the qualities needed to find space for themselves in this new Pacific era, just as faith in their purpose propelled American immigrants from Europe across the Great Plains and the Rockies into the sunny valleys of California in the nineteenth century.

Besides, the Pacific history of the United States is too long to admit of any turning back now. America has had a Pacific coastline since 1819. Long before that, beginning with the very first American census in 1790, the center of gravity of the U.S. population had been moving relentlessly westward, away from the Atlantic and toward the Pacific. In 1790, that central point was 12 miles east of Baltmore, Maryland. Today, it is just west of DeSoto, Missouri, 970 miles closer to the Pacific. In the nineteenth century, Americans coined an unequivocal term for their sense of westward expansion, namely, "Manifest Destiny." The phrase, of course, has some unpleasant connotations, for it was used to gloss over or even justify a multitude of injustices toward American Indians in the settlement of the West, and later a sometimes cavalier attitude toward any obstacles seeming to stand in the way of the expanding American presence in the Pacific Ocean.

Fundamentally, though, Manifest Destiny was a label for an unconscious sense of American energy and drive already apparent in action rather than a witting rationale for preconceived conquest.

Even the missionaries who brought the Christian faith (and literacy, too, it should be remembered) to Hawaii sailed there on merchant ships long familiar with Pacific waters. American whalers, merchants, missionaries, and sugarcane growers transformed Hawaii (neither wholly beneficially nor wholly maliciously) between the death of the first king of all the islands, Kamehameha I, in 1819, and the 1890s. By the time the Hawaiian Islands were annexed in 1898, the United States was already taking over the Philippines from Spain. All of a sudden, the United States, in its rush to assume a political role in the world commensurate with its size and economic muscle, reluctantly found itself a colonial power as well. The consequences of that decision are, in a manner, still being played out today in the Philippines.

The great American bond with the Pacific and the countries and peoples within it and at its farthest edges has, of course, had moments of great stress and anguish. The United States has fought three wars in the Pacific in the past fifty years. The first of these, World War II, was with Japan, a renascent, newly invigorated and industrialized state that might have emerged from its sleep of isolation from the world several decades later than it did but for the restless ambitions of nineteenth-century American traders and explorers. The second of the three wars, in Korea, was in part a consequence of the falling out by the major world powers, the United States and the Soviet Union, over how to fill the gap left by Japanese imperialism in Korea.

As for the most recent of the Pacific wars in which America was involved, the long conflict in Vietnam from 1962 to 1975, there have been unexpected blessings amid the hot coals of anguish. It remains a truism that the American mistakes in that war grew out of a failure to understand the limits of U.S. power as a whole. But it is equally true that the American decision to intervene in Indochina stemmed from an almost unconscious belief that the future of the United States, more than that of any other major power in the world, was inextricably bound up with the overall fate of Asia. Interestingly, Vietnam, its Laotian satrapy, Khmer Rouge–controlled Cambodia, and xenophobic North Korea — all Communist states, of course — were the only countries in Asia that drew any comfort at all from the American defeat or saw it as a harbinger of American withdrawal from Asian affairs. The rest of the region, including the People's Republic of China, knew it was no more realistic, and no less foolish, to expect the United States to wash its hand of the affairs of the Pacific Ocean than to expect it to cut off its links with Western Europe.

The Chinese attitude in particular toward the American Pacific presence over the past 150 years tellingly confirms this. China's relationship with the United States has been volatile on both sides of the Pacific, but the truly positive aspects have their roots in an aspect of nineteenth-century American foreign policy in Asia that tended to be forgotten in the noise and recriminations surrounding the U.S. role in Vietnam. More than in any other region of the world in which the United States has been involved, idealistic motives and the American sense of being the keeper of a revolutionary democratic tradition have constantly erupted through the surface of mere national strategic interest. It was a cardinal American belief in the last century, and in much of the present one, that free trade and the general progress of civilization went hand in hand, as much in the Pacific as in any region of the world. For this reason, U.S. governments tried long and hard throughout most of the nineteenth century to prevent the spread of European colonialism into new regions in Asia.

The Chinese themselves never doubted this. American diplomacy in the nineteenth century was studded with attempts to boost the dignity and international stature of the then-crumbling Qing (pronounced "ching") Dynasty regime. The Chinese acknowledged this aspect of U.S. diplomacy by appointing the first American envoy to Peking, Anson Burlingame, as their government's own official representative in a diplomatic mission to the West in 1867. It was first to the United States, also, that the Qing Dynasty began sending out officially selected delegations of students to acquire Western technology and skills. Later, when former physician Sun Yat-sen led a republican revolution that overthrew the Qing regime, it was American-originated ideas of democracy, national independence, and popular welfare that inspired his movement. Where had Sun got his ideas? Primarily in Hawaii, where he had attended an Anglican mission school, become a Christian, and entered upon a lifelong belief in the efficacy of democratic principles and the notion of progress as keys to solving China's problems. Today, in recognition of the value of American education historically in the building up of China, some 12,000 students from the People's Republic are currently studying in American universities.

Even before the 1911 Revolution in China for which Sun Yat-sen worked, America's Pacific presence had been accepted — as a beneficial phenomenon — by the two emerging rivals in the north-western sector of the ocean, Russia and Japan. For agreeing to act as an intermediary in the peaceful conclusion of the Russo-Japanese War of 1905, President Theodore Roosevelt in 1906 became the first American to be awarded the Nobel Peace Prize. How fitting that Roosevelt's conviction of America's Pacific stake should have been acclaimed in a way that testified to his country's peaceful intent in the area!

Historically, the message is clear: America has always had a Pacific destiny, and it has overwhelmingly acted in the noblest traditions of national idealism. Even the hardest of the United States's Pacific experiences, the Vietnam War, had unanticipated benefits, buying time for much of the region, especially the ASEAN countries, to build up their economies and societies, and tying down the energies of Communist North Vietnam in one relentlessly focused struggle to impose its will on the South. An alternative path might have been an unchallenged Hanoi emerging as a re-gional Communist superpower. In looking back upon their Pacific history, therefore, Americans have much to be proud of, just as, in looking forward, they have much to be optimistic about in facing the Pacific Rim's challenges and opportunities.

There is little doubt that the leaders of American business have already grasped the extraordinary significance of the United States within the Pacific Rim community. The U.S. investment in South Korea, Hong Kong, Taiwan, the Philippines, and even in China, not to mention the two-way trade volume with these countries, Japan, and others, reflects this. Inexorably, the United States is being propelled into an ever-closer relationship with its commercial and diplomatic partners of East Asia. More and more, too, what the leaders of American business have sensed will filter down to small companies, often precisely those with the flexibility, originality of ideas, and energy to move quickly into new market areas. The Pacific Rim is indeed being changed before our eyes. But along with the challenges brought by change are opportunities that have rarely arisen before for adventurous Americans.

2

KOREA

No Calm in the Morning

THE CITY OF SEOUL, capital of the Republic of Korea, sprawls rudely atop and around the hills that look down on the Han River. It is a boisterous, bustling city, higgledy-piggledy with the headlong growth of the past twenty-five years, a patchwork of neighborhoods, industrial concentrations, luxury hotels, two-story family sweatshops, and, in the past half-dozen years, soaring office towers, the status symbol of big-time finance in every business downtown around the world. Amid all this, meanwhile, there is a new Seoul slowly arising. It is the Seoul of the 1988 Olympic Games. The ugly mudflats of the Han River are being dredged. New highways are under construction that will sweep alongside the banks of the Han into the vast Olympic complex. The city, in a word, after its frenzied ride to success, is donning respectability. By the time the Olympic torch is lit on September 18, 1988, Seoul will not really have become a carefully planned city, as its much smaller northern rival, Pyongyang, in an austere sort of way, manages to be. It will nevertheless be impressive enough to visitors, and convince them that Korea, once the "Hermit Kingdom" and the "Land of Morning Calm," has leaped conspicuously into the community of major world nations.

Impressive in this sense, without question, is what all South

Koreans want their city to be two years hence. In very much the same way that the Tokyo Olympics in 1964 symbolized for Japan both its forgiveness by the world for the war and its acceptance as a major nation once again, so 1988, Koreans hope, will be the year in which their nation is recognized globally as a truly significant one. Seoul itself, a pile of ugly devastation only thirty-two years ago, will aspire to be an emblem of Korea's own emergence into economic and diplomatic prominence on the world scene. The city was selected in 1981 by the International Olympic Committee as the successful bidder for the 1988 Games for several reasons. One was that the Seoul Sports Complex, an Olympic-quality ensemble of buildings that will be the heart of the competitive events, was already under construction. Another was the desire for the Games to be held in a developing country, preferably in Asia. A third was strong evidence of Korean ability to organize effectively and to complete appointed tasks within deadlines.

Americans, on the whole, have been slow to recognize Korea's growth into an important economic power, a fact that causes considerable annoyance among most Koreans. Perhaps hazy memories of the destitute place that Korea was at the end of the Korean War have contributed to their fuzzy ignorance; or perhaps they notice only the "Made in Korea" labels on stuffed animal toys and Christmas trinkets. In any event, the economic facts of Korea's world status are ample rebuke to such misperceptions.

With a population of 42 million — slightly more than Spain's at 38 million — and a land area just larger than the state of Indiana, South Korea is the largest of East Asia's NICs. It is also, with a total foreign trade in 1984 of some $30 billion, the world's fifteenth largest trading nation. Korea's two-way trade with the United States in 1984, at $17.35 billion, secured for it seventh place among America's world trading partners. Significantly, too, the United States had an overall trade deficit with Korea in 1984 of $4 billion. Korea's GNP in 1985 was $83 billion and its per capita national income approximately $2,100. This, of course, put it at the very top of the league of developing countries, as well as making it a front-runner, along with the three other NICs, Taiwan, Hong Kong, and Singapore, in the breakthrough into the ranks of the developed nations.

To be appreciated properly, the Korean economic achievement today needs to be compared with the state of the country at the end of World War II and, even more starkly, at the end of the Korean War. Under the Japanese, who annexed the whole of Korea in 1910 and used it during the 1930s and 1940s as a source of food and manpower to fuel their imperial ambitions in East Asia, Korea had no control whatever over its economic, cultural, or political destiny. For both northern and southern parts of the country, the first taste of true national sovereignty did not come until the end of World War II. Yet for South Korea, freedom from the Japanese brought no economic benefits whatever. The U.S.– Soviet agreement in 1945 to supervise the disarming of the Japanese in two zones, north and south of the thirty-eighth parallel, resulted in a lopsided division of economic resources. Coal and other minerals were found almost exclusively in the north. In addition, some 85 percent of power generation and 65 percent of all heavy industry were located in the northern part of the country.

The Korean War that began in June 1950 only prolonged this imbalance. Both parts of the peninsula were devastated during the hostilities, and the war naturally made any serious economic development hard to implement. Yet even the armistice of 1953 appeared to change matters little. In spite of extensive amounts of U.S. aid (some $13 billion to date, half of it in economic assistance), by 1961, eight years after the end of the conflict, Korea's per capita GNP amounted to a paltry $82 annually. Its balance of payments, moreover, had been in permanent deficit since 1948, when the Republic of Korea officially came into existence. South Korea's total exports for 1961 were $43 million. Imports, by contrast, were four times this figure.

A series of Five-Year Plans, initiated in 1962, began to improve this situation rapidly. The change in direction was made possible by the firm political control of President Park Chung Hee, who had come to power through an army coup the previous year. Park opted for an outward-looking development strategy rather than the alternative based on import substitution. For a nation that had been sealed off from foreigners for centuries, it was a bold decision. Thus, despite its historical precedents, the government began to encourage extensive foreign investment and aggressive foreign trade efforts. Domestic savings were further boosted by bank deposit interest rates paying more than 20 percent. The results of these policies quickly became evident. In the 1961–1971 decade, for example, exports increased at an annual rate of 36 percent, possibly one of the fastest export growth rates for any country in history. The GNP growth rate began to soar, averaging 8.2 percent annually for the next twenty-three years, despite the trauma of 1980. That was the year when President Chun Doo Hwan took power in a military coup, radical students revolted and were brutally crushed by the army in Kwangju, and a harvest proved disastrous — all contributing to a serious economic setback. The country's economy actually shrank in size, for the first time since 1948, by a factor of 5.2 percent.

Throughout the 1962–1984 period, nevertheless, the combination of U.S. aid and broad access to U.S. markets proved decisive for Korea's economic leap out of poverty. In the past half-dozen years alone, for example, Korean trade with the United States has grown at an annual rate of 25 percent, well above the already impressive growth rate for Korean exports as a whole of some 9 percent. In 1984, U.S. purchases of $10.5 billion amounted to 36 percent of all Korea's exports. Trade, in turn, fueled economic growth as a whole. One-third of the $83 billion 1985 GNP figure, for example, came out of foreign trade, a truly astonishing percentage for a country with a relatively large population. Of great concern for Korean economists, however, was the fact that a full 23.5 percent of all Korea's exports earnings were in textiles, a sector heavily threatened by protectionist action not only in the United States, but in the European community as well.

Korea's remarkable climb up from such a modest economic starting point two decades ago was not the product of good policies alone. The Koreans, it has been said, make the Japanese look lazy. Today, Korean workers routinely work five and a half or six days a week, and frequently toil during day shifts for up to twelve hours. Labor union representation, not surprisingly, has been erratic, a fact that clearly stems from Korea's authoritarian political context. Yet, as visiting Americans have often discovered, an intense nationalistic drive to propel Korea into the ranks of major nations of the world, along with a sense of pride at having started with nothing, has also inspired Korean business to entrepreneurial boldness and dash not matched even in Japan. Cho Sooho, vice-president of Korean Air, succinctly expressed this mood in a discussion with one visitor. Cho explained: ''The people running Korean Air today picked themselves up from the ashes of the Korean War. It's a generation that didn't have anything and they were hungry enough to go for it. They know what being hungry is all about. That, coupled with the Confucian ethic and a harsh climate, makes people tough. It explains the Korean drive.''

That drive has expressed itself in the building of major infrastructure projects across the Middle East by Korean construction companies, in the earning of valuable foreign currency by skilled Korean workers both there and in other parts of the world, and in the zeal of many Korean entrepreneurs to have the most modern possible technology for their country's economic development. Already, in fact, Korea boasts the world's largest and most advanced automated steel plant, in Pohang, sixty miles from Pusan. The plant, constructed in 1970, turns out 9.1 million metric tons of raw steel every year.

The steel industry, in turn, has spurred on Korea's shipbuilding industry. From start-up less than three decades ago, Korea today accounts for 15 percent of all the new ships being built in the world. The steel industry has also formed the backbone of what may well turn out to be one of the most intriguing economic challenges to Japan from any Pacific Rim country, namely, Korea's current plunge into automobile manufacture and exports.

Two of Korea's largest corporations are already well placed to carve out important niches in the import automobile market in North America and Western Europe. Other companies may well follow suit. In 1984, for example, the Hyundai company dipped its toe modestly into the Canadian market with its $5,000 sub-compact called the Pony. To the company's surprise and delight, sales shot up to 25,000 within months, exceeding by four times the company's expectations. Early in 1986, Hyundai's Excel model, also a subcompact, began to be available in the American market. Despite likely competition from the Yugo, an extremely low-priced Yugoslav car, the Excel, retailing at about $6,000, is in a position to make deep inroads into the U.S. inexpensive import market. Daewoo, Korea's fourth largest corporation, with annual sales of $7.9 billion, will enter the American market in 1987, but under a well-planned distribution agreement with General Motors. By early 1987, the company plans to begin shipping the first of 70,000 to 80,000 cars annually to the United States, all of them bearing the Pontiac name to avoid protectionist dangers.

Neither Daewoo nor Hyundai is yet in a position to challenge the Japanese in automobile construction from the point of view of engineering quality or overall technological levels. As many Korean businessmen have pointed out to foreign visitors, however, Korea's low labor costs give Korean corporations significant advantages over foreign competitors. This is especially true of the automobile business. A University of Michigan study in 1984, for example, showed that while it cost $24 an hour to build a car in the United States and $12 in Japan, it required an astonishingly low $2 per hour to build a car in Korea. Korean automobile workers, moreover, seem willing to work — or don't have the political clout to protest — longer hours overall than do their Japanese or U.S. opposite numbers. At both Hyundai and Daewoo, for example, the average shift length is ten to twelve hours. In Japan, it is nine to ten hours, and in the United States eight hours.

Korea's ability and willingness to challenge the markets of the rest of the world in such fields as steel, shipbuilding, cement, and automobile manufacturing are bold yet sound approaches for a country with a highly educated labor force. Korean literacy is now virtually universal for anyone under fifty, making possible the development of high-technology industry comparable with that of the advanced Western countries, but without their high labor costs.

Yet the policy poses dilemmas for Korea's economic managers. For one thing, it creates the image of Korea as an already developed country at a time when, as Koreans themselves protest, per capita national income is still only one-third that of Singapore and one-fifth that of Japan. Korea's business leaders themselves tell foreign visitors that Korea is still only a "beginner" country in economic development. The statement is true if Japan is used as the standard, but patently false if the vast majority of the world's developing countries are used as an average. Even more distressing for Koreans, though, their country's very success in areas that have been so dominated in Western markets by the Japanese has invited inevitable comparisons between Korea and Japan.

For the Koreans, who have suffered more from the Japanese than from any other foreign country ever since the attempted invasion of Korea by the Japanese warlord Hideyoshi in 1592, the comparison is particularly invidious and resented. Dr. Kim Kihwan, director general of the International Economic Policy Council of the Government Economic Planning Board, spoke forcefully on this topic late in 1985 in a discussion of Korea's economy. "As Koreans," he explained, "we do not like to be compared with Japan in any aspect." He pointed out that, unlike Japan, which amassed each year a huge world trade surplus, Korea in 1984 had accumulated a trade deficit of nearly $1 billion. Besides, he added, Korea did not, as he claimed the Japanese routinely did, practice "industrial targeting" of exports to import-prone countries. Several Koreans, including opposition figures, have told Americans that they felt their country was being made a scapegoat for the poor trade practices of Japan. The most forceful speaker, however, is President Chun Doo Hwan himself, who has complained that some Americans make no distinction between Koreans and Japanese.

Chun said he had made the same point to President Reagan during Reagan's visit to Korea in November 1983, and claimed that Reagan had gone out of his way to indicate that he was personally well aware of the differences between Japan and Korea in relation to U.S. trade issues. To American visitors in late 1985, though, a senior Korean political figure stressed two specific areas where he said the Korean economy was far more vulnerable than Japan's. The first, he said, was the country's international debt. The politician did not mention the numbers involved, but at $43 billion, the Korean debt is the fourth highest of any individual country in the world. The second, he noted, was that Korea was forced to spend some 6 percent of its GNP on military defense. Japan, by contrast, he said, spent less than 1 percent. The highly placed Korean concluded his disclaimer vis-à-vis Japan with a vivid metaphor. "I would say," he observed, "that if Japan is an M.I.T. professor, South Korea is a sixth-grader in the New York public school system."

If so, the sixth-grader shows signs of resentment not only of the M.I.T. professor, but also of his own elementary school teacher. Many visiting Americans, for example, have picked up strong overtones of irritation with the United States over the issue of Korea's alleged protectionist trade policies against American imports into the country. The irritation was expressed, once again, uniformly by both government and opposition figures. In fact, some of the strongest expressions of displeasure with the United States over this theme has tended to come from opposition leader Lee Min Woo, chairman of the New Korea Democratic party. In a chillingly formal question-and-answer session with U.S. visitors during a 1985 meeting, Lee went on the offensive against the United States. The biggest problem in the protectionist area, he said, was not Korea at all, but Japan. "Still and all," he complained, "the U.S. persists in zeroing in on us Koreans. Do you call this fair? Not I or any of my countrymen do. . . . I can't understand why you are putting such pressure on Korea to open its markets. I don't know whether you consider Korea fragile or what, but this situation is too much to put up with."

For Lee's visitors, it was a tense moment in which the latent anti-American motif of some of the Korean political opposition came clearly to the surface. But American business executives in Korea have plenty of beefs of their own about Korean protectionist habits. American cigarette manufacturers, for example, regularly take Koreans to task for their country's exclusion of foreign tobacco. Other American executives have commented on no less egregious Korean protectionist tendencies. Foreign insurance companies, they claim, have been almost totally excluded from Korea, as have foreign movies. In 1984 only twenty-six foreign movies of any kind (twenty-one of them American) were allowed into the country.

These gripes, legitimate though they are, should nevertheless not be taken out of context. The Korean government has made strenuous efforts to liberalize its investment policies for a decade or more. In 1980, it permitted 100 percent foreign equity ownership for the first time. Foreign banks today also have direct access to the discounting facilities of Korea's Central Bank. Very few other countries, especially in the developing world, have been this open to foreign finance's participation in their markets.

In response, Korean officials defend the tobacco monopoly on the grounds that it has been in place for a century and that 8 percent of all government revenue is derived from its profits. They admit that the Korean government's record of keeping Korean markets inaccessible for foreign trade has not been "entirely clean and impeccable." Yet they argue that the situation is improving all the time. "Since 1980," one Korean economist asserted in a discussion in the fall of 1985, "the country has been inaugurating liberal economic policies on all fronts." He drew attention to the reduction of import tariffs since 1980 from 30 percent to 20 percent and to the absence of any prior licensing requirement for all but 7.7 percent of imported goods. By 1990, the official predicted, that figure would be down to a minuscule 5 percent. By contrast, he argued, in 1980, 69 percent of all imports into Korea had required import licenses before they could be brought into the country. Since Korea had traditionally been isolated for so long from the rest of the world, the Korean economist summed up, it was unfair and unreasonable of the United States to demand that Korea immediately remedy all of its exclusionary trade barriers.

The antiprotectionist barrage being thrown at U.S. visitors to Korea was echoed by a South Korean leader in a talk with American business leaders late in 1985. This Korean, however, turned the problem around. Instead of complaining about U.S. efforts to force open the Korean market in order to admit more U.S. products, he worried aloud at the possibility of further exclusion of Korean products from the U.S. market. "What is happening," he observed quietly, "is a matter of great concern. Who would like to see a trade war? Who would like to see the free world fall? The Communists' attempt to force upon us an alternative [system] is unacceptable to us. If a trade war is to continue, the free world will suffer a setback."

As it happens, the Koreans already have cause for concern at the content of literally scores of House and Senate bills introduced during 1985. One of the most threatening to the economy of Korea and other Pacific Rim countries was the Jenkins Bill, named after Georgia's Congressman Ed Jenkins. The bill called for restrictions on textile imports from Asian countries and passed both houses. It was finally vetoed by President Reagan. Other bills, nevertheless, are waiting in the wings. In the Senate, the Thurmond amendment to the textile bill would single out Korea, Hong Kong, and Taiwan as countries whose textile exports to the United States would be specifically limited. In spite of President Reagan's declaration that he would veto any bill that was "protectionist," Korea, like other Pacific Rim countries such as Taiwan and China, is concerned that the administration, like it or not, will be forced for political reasons to implement restrictions on imports from some countries that are considered particularly discriminatory in their own attitudes toward U.S. imports. Korean economists believe that if these sorts of bills actually become law, their own textile exports to the United States will be reduced by up to 30 percent, costing them perhaps as much as $400 million a year. The bills are dormant for the time being, but are expected to be brought before the House during 1986.

Korea, in fact, has already begun to feel the stiff outer breezes of the threatening protectionist typhoon. It was forced to undergo curtailment of steel sales to the United States under a program of "voluntary" reductions initiated in 1984. Korea also saw its electronics exports eroded by U.S. antidumping regulations against

Korean-made color television sets. Korean economists claim, in addition, that their country loses as much as $4 billion a year in potential export sales because of protectionist laws in some nineteen advanced countries, including, of course, the United States.

The Korean official press has played heavily on the theme, knowing that the issue of national control over the Korean economy is an emotional one for all Koreans, whether they support the government or not. Yet the protectionist issue itself is emblematic of more fundamental developments in the Korean national psyche than mere irritation, however intense, with the terms of international trade. As both foreign residents of Korea and Koreans themselves strongly indicated to Time's Newstour participants, Korea has been sensing its own global coming of age.

One of the most thoughtful observers of this new current is a senior Western diplomat, an academic by background, in Seoul. Speaking eloquently but bluntly at a breakfast meeting to visiting Americans, the diplomat offered the suggestion that many of the commonplace U.S. notions of Korea were "geared for a Korea of twenty years ago and not for a Korea that is undergoing such rapid change." The diplomat said he thought a number of U.S. business and military people entertained stereotypes of Korea's role in Asia that were twenty years out of date. Another embassy officer illustrated this by citing the case of the high-level representative of a major U.S. aircraft manufacturer, who, to make his selling offer sweeter, as he thought, to the Koreans, offered as the clincher the fact that 23 percent of the parts of the plane he was trying to sell had been made in Japan. The senior diplomat explained: "I think we really have to understand this growing, self-assertive nationalism in Korea, because Korea is out at the cutting edge, at the front end of a whole number of countries in this world that are no longer going to just roll over when Uncle Sam says to roll over." He appealed to his audience to work together with U.S. government agencies in export promotion "as never before." He also called for an entirely new effort in the United States to train language and area specialists in Asia equipped to cope with the changing and challenging nature of Korean society. "We need people," he said, "who are going to invest ten years, twenty years in this part of the world and build up contacts which are going to last from generation to generation."

The diplomat's point is a valid one. There is far too little co-ordination between U.S. business and U.S. diplomatic representations in places, particularly in the Pacific Rim, where U.S. diplomatic expertise and contacts can sometimes make a crucial difference to the success of American exports. The fault does not lie completely with either side. American business executives have often found foreign service officers snobbish, remote, and uninterested in the down-to-earth business of making, say, a truck sale. Foreign service officers, conversely, sometimes gripe that American business representatives tend to be uninformed about the countries they are visiting and unfamiliar with customs crucial to successful business.

Both sets of allegations obviously contain elements of truth. If anything, though, and particularly in the Pacific Rim, American business executives surely would improve their performance if they were better equipped linguistically or culturally to deal comfortably with their prospective buyers. While knowledge of a foreign language is not always crucial in view of the international usage of English in commerce — and learning Asian languages in particular usually demands immense investment in time and effort — obviously when the competitive edge in price or quality is slight, an easy familiarity with the culture of the potential buyer might clinch an otherwise uncertain deal.

Neither linguistic nor cultural preparation, however, is sufficient to break through the often quite real barriers of closed markets. The American diplomat's perspectives on Korea's new nationalism were thus listened to with care by his audience, but not with universal sympathy. Many American businessmen have seen their own products systematically excluded from Korean markets by Korea's own protectionist rules. One American businessman, the chairman of a major U.S. manufacturing and technology corporation, privately said later that he had been dismayed by the in-

crease in corrupt tendencies during his own recent business trips
to Korea.

Others have expressed concern about a quite different aspect of
the Korean economy, namely, its huge external debt. The debt
today is about $43 billion, one of the highest in the developing
world. Some business experts believe that this could double in as
little as seven years, and eventually "strangle" the country's economy. American bankers have privately voiced similar concerns.
Though they acknowledge that Korea has a perfect payment record
in regard to its debt, they recall unhappily that several countries
have been forced "over the edge" into bad debt situations because
of economic circumstances over which they had little control. Many
non-Korean analysts of the Korean economy nonetheless assert
that Korea's creditworthiness is actually very good and that its debt
service ratio, at 15.5 percent, is one of the best in the developing
world.

Yet the senior Western diplomat's less than flattering view of
U.S. business efforts in Korea was echoed, interestingly enough,
by some of Korea's top business executives themselves. At a panel
discussion with American visitors, Park Seong Yawng, chairman
of the giant Kumho Group conglomerate, said he thought American businessmen in Korea were "not doing well. They are," he
added, "not trying hard enough to sell in South Korea. At times
I feel South Korea is being at once neglected and ignored by American businessmen. There is a good market here." To rub in this
strong medicine, Daewoo's chairman, Kim Woo Chung, told his
American audience, "You have the capabilities to do a great deal
of business. But you are not active here in Korea. You must be
aggressive." The Kumho Group's Park Seong Yawng had similar
thoughts, and expressed them, if anything, even more sharply.
"You don't look at this part of the world as a potential market,"
he complained to the American businessmen. "You don't send
your salesmen here very often. You ought to be here, but you are
not. I see many CEOs, but only a few of you have facilities here."

The complaints by Koreans about insufficient U.S. business energy in their country carry little weight in those fields where Korean

protectionist measures are tight as a drum: insurance, tobacco, and imported movies, for example. Here, and in other domains, Seoul sets the rules in such a way as to prevent any foreign business enterprises from acquiring a toehold in the market. On the other hand, the charges of a lackadaisical American approach to selling in Korea are valid if other countries are working more aggressively — and with success — to market products that are not disqualified by the high trade and tariff barriers. This, in some measure, appears to be true, certainly in the case of the ubiquitous Japanese. In some respects Korean complaints about the lack of visibility of American business representatives in South Korea are valid: the country is not easy to deal with, has an unpleasant climate, and thus is probably not among the favorite Pacific Rim stopping places of most U.S. business executives.

As to aggressiveness, there has been no absence of that in Korean efforts to expand its exports overseas. Apart from the United States and Europe, with which Korea has diligently sought to strengthen its commercial ties, the new arena for Korea's export ambitions is a surprising one: China. The country that sent a million "People's Volunteers" into combat against South Korean and American troops thirty-five years ago is now eager to do business with one of the fastest-developing countries in the Pacific Rim.

Officially, of course, there is no contact between Peking and the Seoul government. Diplomatic relations are nonexistent between the two countries. As the principal ally and backer of North Korea — the People's Democratic Republic of Korea, to give it its full title — China is publicly obliged to support Pyongyang's claim that South Korea is an illegitimate "puppet" regime whose very existence is propped up by the United States. Yet there is no diplomatic breakthrough that South Korea would rather obtain in Asia than official recognition by China. Seoul would be fully prepared to dump its long-term military and diplomatic relations with the Taipei regime if Peking would confer upon it the dignity of recognition. China, in turn, would be eager to develop relatively close relations with South Korea if it could do so without totally alienating North Korea. It would, for one thing, prefer to defuse the still-worrisome military time bomb represented by the presence of 1.5 million highly armed troops in a state of tense mutual confrontation on the Korean peninsula adjacent to its own territory. But with its perennial long-term perspective on Asia and the world, China is eager to ensure that when the United States eventually withdraws from the Asian mainland, as China believes must take place, no unfriendly element enters the vacuum left by the U.S. departure.

Western diplomats in Seoul privately estimate that two-way trade between China and Korea could total as much as $1 billion a year at present. Most of it is conducted through Hong Kong, with Chinese buyers fully aware of the origin of the products they are purchasing. The Chinese are interested in what the Koreans can show them about high-technology industrial production, about management, and about the overall problems of modernizing an ancient and originally peasant-based Asian economy.

The unofficial business contacts between two Pacific Rim states that are still, technically, in a state of war with each other and eschew diplomatic exchanges is in some respects one of the most quietly encouraging international developments in the Pacific Rim. Though Peking remains in public a loud champion of the cause of North Korea, privately the Chinese have worked behind the scenes to discourage Kim Il-sung or his son and chosen successor from any efforts to reunify the Korean peninsula by force. The Chinese, besides, can read balance sheets. They know that the South Korean economy is one of the most dynamic in East Asia, that South Korean industrial productivity is four times that of China's ally North Korea, and that the gap between the two Koreas is likely to increase further — in South Korea's favor. Currently, North Korea's estimated per capita GNP is approximately $700, barely one-third of the South Korean figure. Yet only twenty-six years ago, in 1960, the relationship was reversed, with North Koreans enjoying a figure of $180 and South Koreans a paltry $75.

For China, which exerted an overwhelming cultural and political influence over Korea from as early as the Han dynasty (202 B.C.–A.D. 220), Korea is a culturally more sympathetic conduit for

Western technology and business skills than is Japan or any Western country. But from the Korean perspective, too, despite the painful experience of Chinese power during the Korean War, China under its reformist leadership has something to offer, especially in the commercial field. Particularly attractive to the Koreans are China's ample resources of raw materials that South Korea needs for its industry but has hitherto had to obtain from Australia, Canada, and the United States. Many U.S. business executives may not have thought through how significant for purchases of U.S. raw materials would be a substantial Korean shift to purchases from the People's Republic.

Daewoo's chairman Kim Woo Chung is typical of a handful of top Korean executives who have visited China and discussed trade opportunities with Peking. During 1985, he visited China no less than five times at the invitation of Chinese ministries interested in doing business with him. The Chinese told him that they would like the Koreans to help them develop their own mineral resources and act as major buyers of them. Kim was noncommittal on whether Daewoo itself was on the verge of major agreements with the Chinese. He nevertheless made it clear that the absence of diplomatic relations between Seoul and Peking posed no problem. He explained that Korean executives were able to enter into joint ventures with China indirectly, using Hong Kong companies as intermediaries.

Another factor in China's preference for big business deals with South rather than North Korea — apart from the obviously greater ability of South Korea to pay its bills — is Peking's own move away from the Stalinist collectivism that still characterizes the Pyongyang economy. Chinese today, at both the official and unofficial level, are often dismayed by the sterile sycophancy of leader deification that characterizes North Korea and its Kim Il-sung cult. For most Chinese, it is an uncomfortable and bitter reminder of their own nightmarish years of political lunacy and the Mao cult during the long Cultural Revolution of 1966–1976. Some U.S. diplomats believe that the best hope for a thaw in the Korean peninsula lies in a realization by Pyongyang, through the Chinese

example, that its 1950s–era state planning monopoly is economically — and in a sense politically — a dead end. If Peking were
ever able to establish diplomatic relations with both Koreas, conceivably the North's conversations with the South might acquire
a tone of realism that has eluded them so far.

In a curiously symmetrical way, Seoul and Peking may also be
drawn toward each other because of the increasing complexity of
the relationships each maintains with its close allies. For China,
little on the surface has altered in the closeness Peking has always
professed to have with Kim Il-sung's regimented regime in North
Korea. The relationship, the Chinese have always noted, is as close
as "lips and teeth." Yet the Chinese are also aware that the temper
of the Pyongyang government is far more in sympathy with that
of the still militantly anti-imperialist Soviet Union than with the
outward-looking, soft-spoken diplomacy characterizing China's
foreign ministry today. Similarly, the declining willingness of many
South Koreans to think of Americans chiefly in terms of Korean
War gratitude has coincided with an evidently growing conviction
that their country now deserves a measure of respect on the international scene.

For both China and Korea, involvement in a new war in East
Asia, particularly in the Korean Peninsula, would be a disaster.
For China, it would be all but impossible to avoid giving support
to North Korea. This would have a devastating impact on the
confidence of foreign investors and could prove a major setback
to China's ambitious program of "Four Modernizations." For South
Korea, it could mean the end of its existence as an independent
state.

Soviet relations with South Korea will doubtless take a long
time to recover fully from the trauma of the shooting down of a
Korean Airlines 747 jet by a Soviet fighter in September 1983.
Meanwhile, the Soviets have not succeeded in thawing the
often frosty relationship they have had with North Korea. The
Soviet embassy in Pyongyang is as isolated from the ordinary life
of North Koreans as are the handful of Third World and neutral

Western countries (Sweden and Austria most prominently). Soviet diplomats, moreover, are no more impressed by the preposterous cult of Kim Il-sung as a great leader of mankind than are their Chinese counterparts. Yet Moscow has made some headway. In May 1984, Kim Il-sung and a large retinue visited the Soviet Union and Eastern Europe for the first time in two decades. In December that year, Soviet Vice-Foreign Minister Mikhail Kapitsa traveled to North Korea for lengthy consultations with Kim and other North Korean officials. Reversing a previous neutrality on North Korea, moreover, the Soviets have in the past two years begun making advanced MiG-23 fighter-bombers available to the Pyongyang regime in return for Soviet military overflight privileges.

Ultimately, though, neither the Chinese nor the Soviets will determine North Korean actions, particularly in relation to the South. With only 19 million people and a mere twenty-four resident foreign embassies in its capital, Pyongyang (Seoul has forty-seven), the People's Democratic Republic of Korea is living out a fantasy notion of its national importance that is both frightening and — thirty-three years after the death of Joseph Stalin — bewilderingly anachronistic. Visitors there find themselves back in an Asian version of the Soviet Union circa 1948, down to the ubiquitous statues and portraits of the leader, the grandiose public works projects juxtaposed with a gray and constricted life-style, the automaton-like predictability of both official and unofficial behavior and speech, even the men's hairstyle — swept straight back from the forehead without a part.

The North Koreans, of course, have taken the cult of personality one step further than the Soviets did under Stalin. Not only does every citizen in public wear a badge with a miniature color portrait of Kim Il-sung, but preparations have long been under way for an orderly handover of power from Kim, seventy-three, to his son, Kim Jong-il, forty-two. As several observers have pointed out, should the transfer of power take place successfully, on or before Kim Il-sung's death, it would be the first case of a Communist dynastic succession. To prepare the minds of ordinary Koreans for it, the regime has for a number of years always referred to Kim Jong-il as "the dear leader," in contrast to his father, invariably known as "the great leader."

Much of this would be merely laughable if the xenophobic misanthropy of North Korea had not been expressed again and again around the world in acts of criminality, violence, and terror. North Korean diplomats have been expelled from several countries for blatant liquor smuggling in enormous quantities. North Korean soccer players in 1982, during an Asian Games elimination match in New Delhi, attacked the referee and had to be physically restrained by Indian police. North Korea has continually acted as a haven and training place for some of the world's most notorious terrorists, notably, according to some reports, the sinister P.L.O. offshoot headed by Abu Nidal.

Far more serious, though, has been the relentless low-level military pressure against South Korea generally and against the U.S. forces stationed there. Easily the most outrageous incident was the attempted assassination of President Chun Doo Hwan by a bomb explosion in Rangoon on October 9, 1983. Though Chun himself escaped, seventeen senior South Korean officials lost their lives. Two North Korean officers later confessed to the killing. Another notorious example of North Korean violence was the ax murder of two U.S. officers by North Korean soldiers in August 1976, in the Joint Security Area at Panmunjom.

Though it would be tempting merely to dismiss Kim Il-sung's violent adventures as the work of a "mad" leader, there is a methodical and, in its own context, entirely rational explanation for North Korea's behavior toward the South. Ever since launching his invasion of South Korea on June 25, 1950, with Soviet knowledge and encouragement, Kim Il-sung has never abandoned his aspiration to rule a united Korea that is fully communized. His total armed force of 885,000 men is the sixth largest in the world. North Korea has an army of 800,000, an air force of 50,000 men that is the third largest in the world in terms of operational aircraft, and a navy of 35,000 that deploys 21 submarines (the third largest submarine fleet in Asia) and more than 330 fast patrol boats. The army alone is 41 divisions strong and has a ranger/commando force of 80,000 that is the largest of any army in the world. The crack troops in this force undergo repeated nighttime training for parachute drops from An-2 transport aircraft, an antiquated Soviet biplane that has come into its own for unconventional warfare because of its ability to fly very low and very slowly. North Korean jet fighter-interceptors number approximately 650. The large majority of these are MiG-15, MiG-17, and MiG-19 aircraft that are obsolescent for air combat but that can still be potent and dangerous in the ground-attack role for which they would most likely be used in a war situation.

The striking aspect of the North Korean armed forces is the overwhelmingly offensive mode for which they have been designed. Between 1974 and 1984, moreover, Pyongyang's military actually more than doubled in size, from 409,000 to the present 885,000. In addition, 65 percent of the North Korean combat forces are on the ground in the southern portion of the country, a large portion of them already pre-positioned in approximately 100 underground fortresses within easy motorized distance of the Demilitarized Zone and South Korea. Almost all of the key ground-force units are now completely mechanized.

North Korean military doctrine, according to defectors and intelligence analysts, is based on the slogan "speedy action, speedy conclusion." An offensive by North Korea, to prepare against which there would be almost no warning time whatever, would aim at rolling up South Korean and U.S. military units in-country in a lightning strike of five to seven days. This would be too fast to permit the United States to mobilize and deploy its own combat forces swiftly enough to turn the tide and prevent complete South Korean defeat. The speed of the offensive, the North Koreans obviously hope, would derive partly from effective behind-the-lines operations by airlifted North Korean commandos, partly from the use of U.S.–built Hughes 500 and 300 combat helicopters in operations of tactical deception. Pyongyang illegally obtained some eighty-seven of these choppers, which are also standard equipment in the South Korean army, through third parties. American intelligence officials believe that in a combat situation, the choppers would be manned by North Korean troops in South Korean uniforms for the explicit purpose of causing maximum confusion and disorder in South Korean rear areas. In March 1985, Deputy Assistant Secretary of Defense James Kelly explained bluntly the seriousness of the North Korean threat to a House of Representatives subcommittee. "The threat North Korea poses to the South," he said soberly, "is greater now than at any time since the Korean War."

There is one thing the United States can and should do to reduce the level of this threat: maintain the greatest possible military credibility in South Korea consistent with a peacetime armed forces establishment. Large numbers of troops are not needed, simply good troops and the positioning of them very close to the line of demarcation between North and South Korea. North Korea will read in the condition and demeanor of the American troops it observes on its own border with the South the strength of American commitment to go to the South's defense if the North attacks. However long it is necessary, however anachronistic the stand-off between the two sides may seem, Washington must continue to display its deterrent of troops in the field in South Korea until the North abandons its war of nerves with the South.

The importance of that visible U.S. military presence in South Korea is nowhere more vivid than at Panmunjom, where elite volunteer troops of the U.S. Second Infantry Division are on permanent alert at what is probably the most tense U.S. military outpost anywhere in the world. The Second Infantry Division is positioned right in the middle of what would be the main North Korean invasion route if hostilities were to break out. Just outside the Joint Security Area (JSA), combat-equipped U.S. infantry squads are under alert around the clock to respond to any incident in the 800-meter-wide zone, the focal point of the Military Armistice Commission (MAC) that oversees the Korean Armistice signed twenty-three years ago.

The JSA is carved out of both North and South Korea astride the 151-mile length of the Demilitarized Zone between North and

South Korea. The two components of the MAC are the United Nations Command and the Korean People's Army/Chinese People's Volunteers. Apart from the United States, Great Britain, Canada, New Zealand, Thailand, and France are still formally affiliated with the U.N. Command in South Korea. At aloof and formal meetings of the commission, two South Korean officers, one American, and one British officer sit across a narrow table from two North Korean and two Chinese officers. The meetings are held in a single-story narrow building and the table sits precisely astride the Military Demarcation Line.

Reenlistment rates among U.S. forces in Korea, especially in the Panmunjom area, are among the highest in the world, which says much for both the high morale and the sense of importance the troops as a whole attach to their mission. The Second Infantry Division is the backbone and chief component of the U.S. military force (39,000 personnel) stationed in Korea as a form of tripwire to deter a Communist invasion. But total South Korean forces amount to only 600,000 men, 40 percent less than North Korea's forces. In addition, the U.S.–R.O.K. Combined Forces Command is outnumbered by the North 3 to 1 in tanks, 4 to 1 in ships (mostly fast patrol boats), and 2 to 1 in artillery. Military planners at U.S. Eighth Army Headquarters in Seoul admit that "early air and naval augmentation forces are critically important" for a successful defense of South Korea against a North Korean attack. The meaning of this is as worrisome as it is obscured by military circumlocution: if reinforcements did not reach U.S. forces in South Korea within hours should the North attack, the Americans might well be wiped out as a fighting unit and the South would fall.

The reality of the threat from the North has been the dominant theme of life in South Korea ever since the Korean War ended nearly a quarter of a century ago. No one is more aware than the average inhabitants of Seoul that the DMZ, across which an attack from the North would come, is only twenty-five miles to the north of their city, a mere four to five minutes for attacking jet aircraft. This fact has given rise to deeply entrenched anti-Communist sentiments among most South Koreans and seriously stunted the development of free democratic institutions. In effect, the constant worry about a Northern invasion has provided the public justification of the perpetuation of a highly authoritarian system of government since the Republic of Korea came into existence in 1948. Since then, the country has had only four presidents, and all but the first, Synghman Rhee (1875–1965), came into power by military coup. Many, perhaps most Koreans would actually feel insecure and uncomfortable if democracy suddenly broke out without any commensurate lessening of North-South tensions. Several others, though, feel themselves suffocating under the current political status quo.

Korea's president today, former general Chun Doo Hwan, rules through a system that is authoritarian but not dictatorial. Opposition parties were permitted to form themselves in time for elections for the 276-seat unicameral National Assembly in February 1985. The main opposition party, the New Korea Democratic party, headed by veteran opposition figure Lee Min Woo, did unexpectedly well, winning 102 seats. This performance raised the hopes of political change once more among such veteran opposition figures as Kim Dae Jung, sixty, who has survived a kidnapping from Tokyo to Seoul by Korean CIA agents (1973) and a death sentence for sedition by President Chun (1980), and his increasingly visible colleague, Kim Young Sam, fifty-seven. Both Kims are co-chairmen of the Council for the Promotion of Democracy in Korea, a group that lobbies, within the limits of the law, for the emergence of a much more democratic system of government than exists at present.

Lee and the two Kims have complained angrily to visiting Americans about President Chun's rule, about the existing constitution (which guarantees an end to the rule of President Chun in 1988, but makes no provision at that time for new elections), and about the U.S. role in South Korea. Kim Young Sam warned a group of U.S. visitors late in 1985: "I sincerely hope that the President will follow the spirit and provisions of the new constitution. If he fails to do so, we are bound to see uprisings break out around the country. The outcome then will be a second Vietnam." Lee Min

Woo was even more radical, predicting that if President Chun did not make arrangements to change the constitution and permit direct popular election of the next president, his opposition party would have "no alternative but to start a national campaign for constitutional change."

In a statement that sounded somewhat odd to his listeners, Kim Dae Jung insisted that the U.S. military commander in Korea should actually intervene to "prohibit" the Korean military from trying to influence Korean politics by sheer force. "If the [U.S.] Combined Forces Commander wants to help in Korea," Kim somberly intoned, "he should remember what happened in Vietnam." Kim later explained that he meant that rule by the military in Vietnam had led to corruption and disaffection with the government for a large part of the population, and that this was what might happen in Korea also. He suggested that U.S. troops might be able to compel, say, Korean army units bent on seizing power, to stay in their barracks. But he offered no realistic suggestion as to how 39,000 U.S. troops might be able to control the actions of several hundred thousand R.O.K. troops in their own country.

Even less realistic to Americans visiting South Korea in October 1985 were suggestions by Kim Young Sam that the fragile ongoing dialogue between North and South Korea, conducted intermittently at Panmunjom, should be "realized by all the Korean people." Some listeners thought he had in mind a sort of "flower power" movement of Northerners and Southerners toward national reconciliation. However unlikely such a notion might seem in the South, it would be laughable to imagine its implementation in the militaristic and regimented North. In a similar vein, Kim Young Sam proposed that North Korea would be "deterred" from attacking the South if there were really a high degree of democracy in South Korea. It is arguable, though, whether North Korea's notoriously quirky international behavior is ever likely to be influenced by other countries' moral rectitude.

The United States has, in fact, played a role in Korean politics, but in a quiet, low-key way. Pressures from the U.S. Embassy, for example, were largely responsible for preventing the execution of

Kim Dae Jung in 1980 and for the considerable degree of freedom that he has experienced since returning from a brief period of self-exile in the United States in February 1985. Ironically, though, and despite a tendency of some of Korea's more radical students to equate their own government's authoritarianism with its U.S. alliance, the American ability to influence the overall course of political events in Korea is severely limited. An American diplomat commented in 1985: "There's a misperception that the U.S. runs things in Korea. That day has long gone."

It should not, of course, return. But the United States's relative powerlessness to affect events in South Korea in a truly significant way will challenge the skills of Washington policy-makers and Seoul-based diplomats. Given the obvious need for the United States to continue its strong economic relations with South Korea, to what extent should the United States swallow its distaste for the sometimes heavy-handed authoritarianism of the Chun regime? In addition, given the ever-present Northern threat, should the United States largely refrain from trying to nudge Seoul back toward political freedom in case a sudden outburst of pent-up feeling leads to a disastrous destabilization of the South?

There are no hard-and-fast answers to these queries. In the long run, there is no question, even in Asia, that democratic regimes are more stable than right-wing authoritarian ones, which often operate by unclear rules that they themselves modify as they go along. Very few countries, though, have had to make their transition from dictatorship to democracy in the face of such a close enemy threat as that which faces Korea. It is unquestionably in U.S. interests to see the Seoul government give way to a stable and popular democratic regime. But it would be sheer folly for Washington to set a return to parliamentary democracy in South Korea as a higher priority for its diplomacy in Seoul than continued maintenance of the fragile armistice along the DMZ. In a war, everything in South Korea would be likely to be lost.

As an unstated condition for treading very gently upon Korean political sensibilities, the United States should nevertheless lean strongly on Seoul to abandon the more egregious of its protectionist tendencies. Korea is indeed not Japan in protectionist terms, as Koreans repeatedly insist. But neither is it Hong Kong. Korea's continuing prosperity has been made possible by U.S. market generosity. It is certainly time for the Koreans to be reminded by the United States, again and again, if necessary, of the need to reciprocate.

While working behind the scenes to this end, meanwhile, the United States should do everything publicly to support South Korea's growing aspirations to full international recognition. With the Asian Games scheduled for Seoul in 1986 — essentially a dry run for the Olympics — the country is well on the way to achieving this goal. Anyone who has seen the graceful, 100,000-seat Olympic Stadium, with its neat, color-coded seating and its clean appearance, can have no doubt that the Koreans are well able to organize superbly the Olympic games. Most of the facilities are completed already. Minister of Sports Lee Young Ho explained his country's self-confidence about the entire 1988 project. "When we go into the Olympic Games in 1988, we will go in better rehearsed than any other country."

He is probably right. But Lee Young Ho also reminded American visitors during 1985 just how seriously the Koreans are regarding their Olympics as an emblem of national achievement. In an unusually candid and off-the-cuff speech to his business guests, he explained: "We want to prove something to ourselves through the Olympics. We want to prove to ourselves that there are reasons for further hard work so that when we meet the twenty-first century, we shall have something to bring our grandchildren, not as a burden, but as a blessing." Earlier in 1985, President Chun had made a similar speech about Korea's future, revealing the same sense of national pride. He was speaking about Korea's role in the twenty-first century. "The new century as I envision it," he explained, "will be the century of the Korean people. As a most advanced nation, Korea will lead the age of the global village. . . . My firm belief is that by that time, Korea will have attained a Gross National Product of $250 billion, or $5,000 per capita GNP. This means that Korea will have grown into the fifteenth largest economy in the world and the tenth largest trading country. By that time we will have firmly established a tradition of peaceful changes of government and will have become rich enough to be a creditor to foreign countries."

If Korea had not already achieved formidable targets on its path to national economic development, Chun's words might be dismissed as so much Third World demagoguery. Yet there are few Koreans, whether of the government or the opposition, who would take issue with these aspirations, even if the forecasts themselves assume the best of all possible circumstances between now and the magic year 2000. In a very ordinary sense, Chun's sentiments express a nationalism that has grown up in the wake of visible economic achievement. It is, moreover, a nationalism that is hardly unique to Korea. Today, it is increasingly in evidence in the view of the world exhibited by Korea's former Confucian mentor, China, seven years after China's reform program came into existence. In both countries, handling nationalism wisely will be a supreme challenge to the intelligence and sensibility of American businessmen, diplomats, journalists, and educators. In the twenty-first century, Korea will continue to make waves.

For Americans keenly interested in South Korea as a new location for trade, neither this new nationalism nor the obvious concerns about security should distract them from appreciating one fundamental point about the country: its economic — and thus its international trade — potential remains enormous. With its skilled and highly literate labor force, its immense social self-discipline, Korea offers especially welcome conditions for direct equity investments by U.S. companies. For the foreseeable future, too, there will be many fields in which its own technology has not caught up with its economic needs: aviation, advanced weaponry, medicine, to name but a few. In many of them, the United States is the only logical supplier, and in some, the only trusted one. As Koreans sometimes like to point out to Americans, their country's economic success during the past two decades has been America's. This assertion alone should enhance U.S. resolve, in spite of the uncertainties, to consider South Korea one of the better investment opportunity locations of the Pacific Rim.

3

CHINA

The Rush to Modernization

"WE ARE TRYING to compress the industrial revolution, the Renaissance, and the Reformation into one decade." — Ying Ruocheng, China's leading actor and director.

The comment, of course, is an exaggeration. To many Chinese it nevertheless expresses the reality of what China has been undertaking for the past seven years under the regime of Deng Xiaoping, China's de facto leader during this time. For Americans, the novelty of China's extraordinary transformation, beginning in 1979, from a xenophobic, vituperatively anti-Western, egalitarian-obsessed society into an outward-looking state in search of global status and prestige may have worn off somewhat. Big Bird and Bob Hope have been to China. President Reagan has been to China. A lot of people's aunts, cousins, bosses, and colleagues have by now been to China. They come back with stories of friendly faces, of attractive Chinese girls wearing designer jeans and boots, of American movies on Chinese television, of ultra-modern hotels and the acceptability of the American Express card. Since so many people have seen all this, it is no longer to be considered exceptional.

For all its growing familiarity to Western minds, however, China's single-minded pursuit of modernization for the past seven years is one of the most important developments in all of Asia in this century. The Communist revolution of 1949 halted a relentless cycle of foreign invasion and civil war that had proceeded, with little interruption, ever since the 1830s. It unified the country and set in motion a nationwide construction of industrial infrastructure. It also forcibly drew the attention of the rest of the world to the fact that China, to use the phrase employed by Mao Zedong in 1949, had "stood up." For a time, too, China's newfound Marxist-Leninist fervor led to the impression that Peking had somehow subordinated its mighty cultural and national heritage to the leadership of the Soviet Union, the preeminent world Marxist power.

Within less than two decades, however, that very ideological fervor had coalesced into a self-destructive and foreign-baiting madness known as the Cultural Revolution. Many people saw the phenomenon, basically lasting from 1966 until Mao's death and the arrest of his leftist supporters, the "Gang of Four," in 1976, as renewed proof that China was lost to the world of rational discourse. In fact, Theodore H. White, one of the most prominent of all American reporters on China in the past fifty years, presided over a television documentary on China in the late 1960s entitled "China: The Roots of Madness." Not only the Cultural Revolution, but a series of nationally destructive political campaigns extending back to the early 1950s confirmed for many people what appeared an obvious point: China was uninterested in establishing normal relations with itself, much less with the Pacific Rim countries or the major powers of the rest of the world.

It is thus all the more remarkable to note that the current reformist policy of Deng Xiaoping is not simply a break with the chaotic years of Maoist egalitarianism, which for three decades dominated the policies of the People's Republic of China. It is a substantial new development in Chinese history. Nearly two years ago, an expert and highly experienced China hand among senior Western diplomats resident in Peking said: "China today probably has the best government it has had in 150 years." The comment is entirely accurate. For the past six years China, nearly one quarter of mankind, has been externally at peace and internally governed by a leadership group remarkable, in terms of the history of the country for the past four or five decades alone, for its consistent policy and cohesive composition. There have been no dramatic purges, no nationwide traumatic political campaigns to endure, no sudden shifts in economic policy or foreign diplomacy. Even if the epoch of Chinese history dominated by China's "paramount leader" — to use the quaint English euphemism Chinese officials apply to Deng Xiaoping, the benevolent gray eminence in Chinese politics — were to be remembered for nothing else, it would be a singular achievement. For observers of the Pacific Rim, it is worthy of extended reflection.

China's size and the grandeur of its historical achievement sometimes blind people to how poor the country has been for the past two centuries, and how low it still ranks among the nations of the world in terms of per capita income. In 1980, the per capita income was approximately $300 a year, comparable with Haiti's, and in the bottom 13.2 percent of the 159 member countries of the United Nations. In Sichuan Province, peasants still use wooden plows and wooden-rimmed wheelbarrows, some two millennia after Chinese peasants, in more prosperous times, were already using metal-tipped plows. The principal beast of burden in many parts of China is still the human being. Peasant youths, straining against a yoke connected to great cartloads of produce or bricks, can still be seen entering from the countryside, for example, the suburbs of Hangzhou, one of China's most elegant cities in one of its richer provinces. In Shaanxi and Gansu provinces, huge numbers of peasants still live in caves, barely eking out an existence from the thin and exhausted soil. Even in the fuliginous cities of the industrialized northeast, millions of urban dwellers exist and toil in a grimy and polluted netherworld, their basic needs of food and shelter met, but their lives punctuated by neither comfort nor variety.

It is against this setting that the unprecedented boldness of China's current policy of "Four Modernizations" should be seen and that a realistic assessment of China's role in the emerging Pacific Rim region should be made. Had it not been for internecine political strife in China in the last half of 1975, the modernizations might have been a decade underway by now. As it is, though they were announced in that year while Mao Zedong and China's Premier Zhou Enlai were still alive, they had to wait for their implementation until the death of both of these men, the arrest of the "Gang of Four" (Mao's wife, Jiang Qing, and Shanghai-based leftist leaders Zhang Chunqiao, Yao Wenyuan, and Wang Hongwen), and the final emergence to preeminent state power of Deng Xiaoping himself some five years later.

The goal of the Four Modernizations is usefully and disarmingly simple. It is to attain the modernization of China's industry, agriculture, science and technology, and military in the shortest possible time. Concretely, the Chinese have set themselves the task of quadrupling the approximate 1979 level of per capita national income to some $800 — in 1979 dollars — by the year 2000. In practical terms, this has meant that China's economy has been required, since 1979, to grow at a consistent, average rate of 7.5 percent. In itself, this is not a farfetched goal. Other Asian economies, Korea and Taiwan, for example, have maintained higher rates of growth for a decade or more at a time. China, however, has predicated its success in modernizing on being able to sustain a balanced growth throughout the economy and on containing the social consequences of income disequilibrium generally prevailing during periods of very rapid economic development. China also believes that all this can be accomplished with minimal changes in the fundamental political structure of the country and without the traumatic social upheavals that have afflicted so many other developing societies.

Interestingly, China's modernization program has been publicly embarked upon by the Deng Xiaoping regime with scant reference to ideology at all, much less to the prevailing official doctrine of Marxism-Leninism. A Western diplomat in Peking comments: "The fundamental thing about the Chinese economy today is that it is based on an objective view of where they are going and an objective view of how to get there. Their goal is not to perfect socialism, but to become a superpower."

The superpower aspirations of China would be no more fervently denied today than by the Chinese themselves, for whom the very term connotes what they call "hegemonism" (usually referring to the Soviet Union's world role) and "superpower rivalry," by which they mean efforts by the United States to counter the world expansionism of the Soviet Union. The Chinese, moreover, are genuinely conscious of their country's poor economic condition. They find it useful to think of themselves as members of the Third World. Partly this is because, by comparison with most Third World countries, China, despite the problems of the 1950s and 1960s, looks rather impressive. Partly, too, the Chinese realize that they cannot secure the continued cooperation of advanced capitalist countries in their modernization if there is widespread international belief that they will soon be in a position to throw their weight around on the world scene. Privately, Chinese diplomats nevertheless occasionally let slip glimpses of a national self-image that contradicts the poor-cousin motif they generally wish to convey. A senior Chinese diplomat in Peking confided to a Westerner more than a year ago: "We are a major power. We feel we have the right to have our voices heard on a wide variety of international issues."

There are three key elements to China's economic reform program: rural reform, urban reform, and an "Open Door" policy toward foreign investment, trade, technology, and skills. In a sense, the Open Door policy is the ultimate key to China's aspirations to become an advanced nation by the middle of the twenty-first century. Even though rural reforms could achieve significant success in the largely backward countryside without a great deal of reference to the world economy, it would be inconceivable for China to modernize its industrial plant and enter the front ranks of world trading nations without learning the basic skills that have assured the international success of other Pacific Rim nations. This idea, clearly, has been grasped by virtually all elements of China's leadership. At the important Third Plenum of the Twelfth Central Committee, in October 1984, the Peking leadership finally launched its long-awaited program for urban reform. The official document emerging from this party gathering affirmed the case for China's openness to the outside world. It stated, "National seclusion cannot lead to modernization." In one sentence, China's political leadership thus discarded the autarkic economic doctrines that had guided China's development policies during the thirty years of the Mao Zedong era.

By October 1984, China had already gained from five years of experience in throwing its doors open to foreign commerce and investment. It had concluded that, whatever the shortcomings of a mass exposure of the Chinese population to foreign culture, the influx of foreign money and technology was having a powerful stimulative effect on many parts of China's domestic economy and the experiment should be continued. Yet the urban reform program itself, delayed for months at least because of opposition to many aspects of it within the party, could never have been introduced at all had China's rural reform not already displayed astonishing success in raising living standards in the countryside.

In a sense, China's rural economy had nowhere to go but up when Deng Xiaoping brought Sichuan governor Zhao Ziyang to Peking in 1979 to oversee this and other modernization programs nationally. Zhao had experimented with a new, locally based "contract responsibility system" in Sichuan in order to increase agricultural production by introducing personal incentives. When the new system was then made mandatory for the country as a whole, its success may well have surprised even its most vocal advocates. The agricultural communes, vast, unwieldy economic units comprised of scores of villages and farms and first established in 1958 at the outside of Mao's Great Leap Forward, were broken down into "townships" at the administrative level, and into production units and eventually family households at the economic level. Peasants were told they must contract with the government for an agreed-upon quota of grain or other produce output at a fixed state price for the year ahead. Anything they produced beyond the contract, however, could be sold either at a premium price to be paid by the state or at whatever price the produce would fetch on the free market. In addition, peasants were permitted to become involved in any "sideline" occupations — such as hog raising or fish farming — that earned them money. They were also allowed to band together economically with others in order to pool capital for the purchase of agricultural implements or vehicles for the more effective marketing of their output.

Almost immediately, the results showed up in national statistics. China's agricultural output has grown by 7.9 percent annually ever since 1979. By contrast, the average annual increase in agricultural production during the 1953–1978 period was a much more modest 3.2 percent. The real income of peasants by 1983, moreover, had almost exactly doubled the 1979 figure. In some parts of China it grew by a multiple of ten or more. In rice-rich Guangdong Province, for example, where clement weather allows for up to three crops a year and cultivation of numerous other crops, several counties had a significant number of family households earning 10,000 yuan ($3,500) a year.

The phenomenon of sudden and considerable family wealth quickly produced its own sobriquet for these households (as so often happens in China). They were called "wanyuanhus," or "ten-thousand-yuan-households." Though there were many parts of China, notably in the impoverished provinces of Guizhou, Gansu, and Shaanxi, not to mention in Tibet, where incomes rose barely a fraction of this amount, the increase in buying power nationally developed a momentum of its own. In Guangdong Province, peasants often bought not just "the Four Big Things" (a color television set, a washing machine, a refrigerator, and a stereo cassette player), but motorbikes, trucks, and even, in a few cases, private automobiles, the very first such items permitted in China since the Cultural Revolution began in 1966. For most peasants, though, these items were less important than a new house. With or without permission, peasants all over China launched a domestic construction boom the like of which may never have been seen in Chinese history. Nearly half of all the peasant houses in China, according to Chinese officials, were in fact constructed between 1979 and 1984.

The incongruous slogan "To Get Rich Is Glorious" was one of several mottoes coined by the government to sanction such formidable rural economic activity, which has shown no signs of abating. The number of privately owned tractors in China, for example, grew from 90,000 to 290,000 during the 1983–1985 period. Yet it was more than slogans that propelled most peasants into a burst of consumerism. Apart from the deliberate dismantling of the communes that accompanied the "contract responsibility system," another powerful sign of commitment by China's leadership to ongoing reform in the countryside was a law introduced in 1984, guaranteeing a fifteen-year usage lease on land made available by the authorities to individual peasant households. Later, this law was further strengthened by a decree authorizing inheritance of the lease by a peasant's heirs. So confident of the success of the rural reforms has China's leadership become that it now permits rural residents to set up businesses with up to 200 employees. The government's ultimate objective: to move 40 percent of China's rural population of 800 million off the land by the year 2000.

Inevitably, the increased purchasing powers of the peasants would have forced China's government to attempt at least analogous reforms in the nation's cities even if the government had not long been aware of the formidable need to modernize Chinese industry and increase productivity. For one thing, as the authorities began to permit peasants to bring their produce into major Chinese urban centers to sell to the townsfolk, city dwellers themselves began to see how well the peasantry had done. Wizened and tanned farmers often annoyed shoppers on Peking's busy Wangfujing Street, the capital's main shopping locale, for example, by swaggering noisily into department or specialized goods stores and buying up expensive consumer items most city residents could only gape at.

China's economic planners, meanwhile, were already alarmed by both the obsolescence of much of China's industry in the early 1980s and the resistance of ordinary workers and state-appointed managers to new ways of working. When the urban reform program was unveiled by the party in 1984, the document describing it was both urgent in its account of the need for major change and soothing in its obligatory rhetorical lip service to the advantages of socialism. Deng at the time cannily denied any direct responsibility for the document's authorship, obviously attempting to tie the label of the reform around the neck of the entire Central Committee. He nevertheless stressed that it would take three to five years for the reforms to begin working effectively and for living standards to start rising as rapidly in the cities as they already had in the countryside.

That caution, as usual with Deng, was well founded. Late in 1985, confirming indirectly that the urban reforms were indeed encountering significant difficulties, Deng was even more cautious in an interview with American business executives about the time needed for the reforms to begin working. "It will take us five years perhaps," he said, "before reforms in the city will work out satisfactorily. So I hope our friends will keep watching very closely. . . . As far as I am concerned, there is no other road for China to take. Other roads would only lead to backwardness." In a separate discussion, Vice-Premier Li Peng, a likely successor to Premier Zhao Ziyang in a year or two, confided that the urban reforms would be "far more complicated" to accomplish than the rural reforms had been.

Leaving aside for the moment the political issues involved, Li is entirely right. The most fundamental of all the issues involved in China's urban reform is the extent to which the economy will free itself of central planning and will be able to function smoothly in close proximity to the international market. The urban reform document of October 1984 promised to reduce the overall domain of central planning with a new system called "guidance planning." In theory, this system will designate through the State Council, China's supreme organ of governmental, as opposed to party, authority, overall decisions for state investment in key areas, but will leave fulfillment of the plan and microeconomic decision-making to the state enterprises themselves. China's 75,000 major state enterprises, for example, will be largely autonomous in operation and will be responsible for their own operational profitability. Peking has bravely announced that it will eventually permit unprofitable factories to go bankrupt, being willing to bear the high, one-shot costs of liquidation rather than the continuing, indeterminate ones of a loss-making enterprise. Meanwhile, the intention is that the enterprises will sign contracts with the government largely in the manner of rural family units. That is, they will be required to turn over a specific quantity of production to the government and will be permitted to make a profit, any way they want, on any production above the specified amount.

This bold move away from central state planning is by far the most ambitious scheme ever attempted in any Marxist-Leninist country to turn back the clock from massive economic centralization to a much more freewheeling system. Success of the scheme, however, is based on the assumption that the same measure of personal incentive that has transformed production in the Chinese countryside will be transferable to the overmanned and at present highly inefficient smokestack industries that comprise the core of China's urban socialism. One of the most outspoken critics of China's centrally planned economic system of the past three decades has been Huan Xiang, director-general of Peking's Center for International Studies. The old system, Huan complained in 1985, "seriously hampered the initiative and creativity of the enterprises and workers and to a great extent emasculated what would otherwise have been a vigorous economy." Then, in a remarkable parallel with a traditional Confucian syllogism, he added: "The more centralized, the more rigid; the more rigid, the lazier the people; the lazier the people, the poorer they are."

Still, Huan himself, like most other Chinese economists today, is obliged to admit that success in freeing up China's urban economy is completely dependent on price reforms. Those reforms, in turn, have never been attempted in any other centrally planned economy in the manner that the Chinese are currently pursuing: that is, allowing prices in some sectors to reflect purely market demand, while strictly controlling them in other sectors. Vice-Premier Li Peng estimates that Peking still fixes prices for 70 percent of the products sold by state enterprises, permitting 30 percent of the products to reflect true economic value. Yet he told American visitors in late 1985 that he hoped the 30 percent figure for non-fixed-price items would increase. The rather stark acknowledgment of the novelty of attempting genuine price reforms when the overwhelming bulk of the Chinese economy is still centrally administered prompted one senior U.S. executive to observe to Li: "You are attempting something unprecedented, a combination of socialism with a free market economy. Frankly, some people in the West doubt that these contradictory forces can in fact be joined."

The free movement of prices in some sectors of the economy has already caused anxiety among many Chinese, particularly those old enough to remember the chaotic inflation in Chinese cities during the late 1940s, the last few years of the Chinese Nationalist regime, the Kuomintang. Some food prices in cities like Shanghai and Peking have risen as much as 40 to 50 percent. More ominously, as some peasants have withheld produce or animals for slaughter from the market in the hopes of obtaining higher prices, there have actually been instances of pork shortages in Peking and other cities. Wages, of course, have also risen considerably over the past three years for some urban workers (though very little for Communist party urban cadres, for example). Many ordinary Chinese nevertheless complain that while prices for consumer durables have actually come down, that is of little help to them in the day-to-day struggle for the necessities of life. "How many times do you buy a color television set?" one Peking cabbie dryly observed to a foreigner.

Within China's rambling bureaucracy, meanwhile, officials — some with enthusiasm, some with annoyance — are getting used to the fact that salaries will no longer be tied primarily to seniority, as in the past, but to rank and responsibility. Li Peng, who acerbically noted that some department heads were actually paid more than government ministers, said that the abolition of this system had "created enthusiasm among government workers and peasants."

What Li is probably more concerned about, though, is whether China's reforms have created similar "enthusiasm" among the business executives from the advanced capitalist countries that Peking has persistently courted in its Open Door policy since 1979. On the face of it, the results of China's commercial opening up to the outside world are impressive. More than 2,000 foreign businesses had invested in China by the end of 1984. Most of this investment was initiated by overseas Chinese, whom China has wooed back with increasing success from the skepticism with which most overseas Chinese observed the Cultural Revolution and other traumatic events in China before that. The total nonetheless includes investments by seventy U.S., sixty-seven Japanese, and forty-two British, French, or West German companies, with most of the money being put up for joint ventures with Chinese organizations. In the first half of 1985, moreover, some 687 new foreign investment projects had been signed with China, a figure almost equal to the entire total for 1984. At least ninety-four of the original 2,000 businesses were wholly owned foreign ventures, including 3M China Ltd., a subsidiary of Minnesota Mining and Manufacturing Corporation.

Many of the foreigners doing business directly in China through joint ventures were lured there by tantalizing visions of China's gigantic potential market, a theme repeated by China traders for two centuries. A few, especially in highly specialized Chinese export areas, have prospered greatly and have been satisfied with the conditions of their business. The successful China traders have tended to focus on small yet significant purchases year after year in products hard or impossible to obtain outside China. Rare Chinese mushrooms or fungus, or certain kinds of animal pelts, for which there is a steady demand in Japan, Hong Kong, or the West, are typical of the product lines in which some foreign buyers have made a lot of money.

Yet a large number of foreign traders resident in Peking, Shanghai, Canton, and a handful of other Chinese cities have been broadly disillusioned with Chinese business practices. They have complained about arbitrary renegotiation of price terms after formal conclusion of a deal, or about massive and unwarranted increases in rentals for office space or about the official fees demanded for Chinese staff hired through the monopolistic state agencies. In September 1985, for example, interpreters' fees in Peking were hiked without warning by 60 percent; drivers' fees increased by 75 percent, to $200 a month. A U.S. banker in Peking, irritated by the pettiness of some of the price gouging, observed bitterly: "What [the Chinese] don't realize is that this is bad business for them. The foreigners will simply build the increased costs into the prices they charge the Chinese."

The Chinese respond, not altogether cynically, that they are charging what the market will bear. What they mean is not that there is a genuine free market inside China from which foreigners may obtain goods and services; they understand that the government maintains a monopoly on the services available for employment by foreigners (who then pay the Chinese service organization a "salary" six to ten times what the individual Chinese actually receives from the organization). They simply assume that most foreign capitalists are not foolish enough to go on taking a loss if they are unable to make ends meet in their China business. Presumably, should something like a mass exodus of resident foreign business personnel take place, the Chinese would lower their official service personnel fees to the point where the foreigners began to come back again.

Some foreign businessmen do not, in essence, disagree with this approach to the obvious annoyances and the heavy costs of doing business in China. They believe that in the long term foreigners are bound to make money, given the enormousness and variety of China's economic needs. Observed one American: "I just don't think most big business in the U.S., or maybe just most business, can afford not at least to be here, to see how it's going, and take their chances on losing a lot of money. This is the biggest part of Southeast Asia we [Americans] are in, if you look into the future." Some foreign business executives, however, have argued that it is not worth the seemingly endless wait in China for something profitable to turn up. Many also believe that several "noneconomic" factors seriously compound standard business calculations in dealing with the Chinese. Personal favoritism by Chinese officials, for example, or political decisions taken at high level to give contract preference to companies from one country over those from another, regardless of economic sense, lend an element of real hazard to doing business in China.

Despite all the complaints, there are clearly some very exciting payoffs for many foreigners, including Americans, ready to try their hand at it. In 1984, China's two-way foreign trade amounted to more than $50 billion, a 23 percent increase over the 1983 figure. More than $7 billion of that amount was with the United States, whose exports to China have grown steadily despite Chinese unwillingness to purchase grain as promised in an official Sino-American grain agreement. From the United States, the Chinese have shown an enthusiasm for high-technology imports, for example, computers, civil aircraft, precision measuring instruments, and oil-drilling equipment.

China's purchases of U.S. goods in this field have been impressively sophisticated and well planned. In 1984 the Chinese bought twenty-four Sikorsky S-70C Blackhawk helicopters for $140 million. The deal was the first Chinese venture into U.S. exports with a military application. Peking has shown great interest in advanced U.S. avionics for their F-8 interceptors, and in TOW antitank missiles. Already, about half of China's domestic and international long-range jet fleet is American. Most of the aircraft are from Boeing, but McDonnell-Douglas is also in the market. Were it not for strict regulations by the Paris-based Co-ordinating Committee for Multilateral Export Controls (COCOM) against NATO exports to Communist countries, the U.S. sales figure for high-technology items would have almost certainly been several million dollars more than it now is. Meanwhile, since Chinese current fascination with the economic advantages of computers shows no signs of flagging, the field remains open for U.S. companies in this area. During 1986, Chinese imports of computer equipment from around the world are estimated to increase by 50 percent over 1985 sales.

But the Chinese have also made some droll purchases. Twenty long black Cadillac limousines showed up in Peking in 1985, for example, complete with cocktail cabinets and passenger reading lights in the back seats. Their purpose: to ease the transport of

American and other foreign executives who might not feel comfortable riding around in a Chinese-made Red Flag or Shanghai limousine, or even in one of the several hundred thousand imported Toyotas and Nissans.

Few serious U.S. businesses would project sales to China on the basis of something as unlikely as a demand for Cadillacs in Peking. Yet it is precisely the unexpected and even bizarre that has drawn many U.S. companies back to China again and again. Chinese negotiators frequently and sensibly counsel "patience" to busy American executives accustomed to quick business agreements after a few days at most of negotiation. Many Americans have left China empty-handed, fuming and disgusted after finding out that what they assumed to be meetings with Chinese officials to conclude a contract were actually only general exploratory sessions. Others have hung around in near-despair, watching competitors come and go for weeks before their "patience" has in fact been rewarded by the signing of a major agreement. There is much planning in China, but very few things can be known for sure in advance.

Unpredictable as Chinese trade officials often are, however, their business judgment is no more infallible within their own country than that of Americans is within the United States. Fashions often affect Chinese evaluation of high-technology purchases. If a large state enterprise specializing in instrumentation learns that a similar factory across town has just bought one particular brand of personal computers, it sometimes will make a similar or identical purchase in order to appear au courant with developments in the industry. Many U.S. computer companies have in fact prospered in China, locating potential customers in obscure and unexpected corners of provinces far from Peking.

American business has done well in China, particularly given the long hiatus in any kind of relationship between Peking and Washington. But Japan's commercial success has been even more impressive. In 1985, China's two-way trade with Japan was $16.57 million, and showed no sign of decreasing. To an extent that other Pacific Rim countries might well envy or at least wish to emulate,

Japan alone has managed to tap into China's gigantic potential consumer market. China is Japan's second biggest customer, for example, after the United States, in consumer electrical items. Increasingly, Japanese-made stereo, TV, VCR, and other consumer electronic equipment is found the length and breadth of the country.

China's government has gone ahead with the traditionally "unsocialist" practice of specifically importing many consumer items partly because it wants to soak up the purchasing power of the newly enriched peasantry and partly because China's own domestic consumer manufacturing industry has been incapable so far of keeping up with the enormous demand generated by the reform program. Japanese cars have been imported into China in such numbers as to become commodity items in a thriving black market. In one of the most remarkable scams involving Chinese officialdom since the Open Door policy was first implemented, Communist party officials on Hainan Island in 1984 spent $1.5 billion illegally importing luxury goods, from color television sets to luxury limousines, some from Germany, some from Japan. With transportation helpfully provided by aircraft from China's navy, many of the imported items were then delivered to distant provinces for sale at considerable mark-ups. Business schools across the United States might applaud such entrepreneurial ingenuity, but the use of state funds for purposes not authorized by the state is considered an extremely serious crime in China, particularly when personal gain is involved.

The Japanese were the first major foreign country to penetrate the Chinese market in a significant way, starting in the late 1970s. As they have done everywhere else in the world, the Japanese in China have undertaken no major ventures without first meticulously studying the market and local conditions. This, however, has earned them no particular friendship among the Chinese, who have watched with dismay as Japanese companies have singularly failed to invest directly in China to the same extent that the Americans have done. More seriously, China's Open Door to Japan has resulted in some unpleasant backlash developments among China's restive student population. In the fall of 1985, for example, students at Peking University pasted anti-Japanese wall posters up on the campus protesting alleged Japanese "economic aggression" against China. Similar protest movements against the Japanese took place in other Chinese cities. In Shanghai, a student at the elite Fudan University explained the prevailing sentiment about Japan among many young Chinese intellectuals. "The Japanese," he said, "are exporting poor-quality goods to China. Cars and other things break down. They are selling us things that are of not high enough quality to sell elsewhere."

Perhaps to avoid this particular form of dumping, as well as to develop their own indigenous, export-producing industry, China's foreign trade officials constantly emphasize their desire to purchase manufacturing technology rather than simply the manufactured goods themselves. At a detailed working luncheon with American business executives in the Great Hall of the People in late 1985, State Councillor for Economic Affairs Zhang Jinfu told his guests: "Don't think only about selling, but think about transferring technology to raise the Chinese ability to produce this technology. While we are purchasing products, we'd also like to purchase advanced technology."

For many foreign companies, this goes against the grain. They are understandably reluctant to provide developing countries with the technology that will generate future competition against their own products. China, moreover, has in the past been less than impeccable in copyright observance, sometimes copying a foreign manufacturing process without license and then exporting the finished products. Peking officials today are sensitive to this concern by outsiders and have made much of new intellectual property laws drawn up and enacted in China in the past three to four years. A more persuasive argument is that China's need for updated manufacturing technology is to supply the badly undersupplied consumer needs of their own vast population. This point has validity. It would be unreasonable to expect China indefinitely to part with precious foreign exchange for the purchase of consumer goods if the manufacturing technology for them were not especially

advanced and were already widely available in several other countries. For American business executives interested in selling to the
Chinese, of course, the key criterion for any technology export
sale — apart, naturally, from any national security considerations — is whether there is any possibility of the technology's ultimately being used competitively against the supplier.

China, meanwhile, has done considerable selling itself. So successful has its rural reform been in stimulating cotton production,
for example, that it has become, in the course of five years, a net
exporter of the commodity. Previously, cotton was China's third
largest import. The Chinese have also produced so much corn,
wheat, and soybeans that they have been able to export to Asian
markets and compete with the United States, South Africa, and
Argentina. For Washington, this has been a double rebuff. Under
a four-year grain purchase agreement with the United States, the
Chinese were committed to have purchased, by the conclusion of
the term of the agreement on December 31, 1984, 6 million tons
of grain annually. Of this amount, 15 to 20 percent was to have
been corn. But by the time the agreement had expired, the Chinese
had bought only 4.33 million tons of wheat and no corn at all.
Altogether, they had fallen short on agreed-upon purchases by
several million tons. American government officials protested vigorously, but had no final recourse short of retaliation in other areas
of bilateral trade. They felt constrained not to do this mainly in
order not to undermine overall Sino-American relations. They also
wanted to impress upon the Chinese the importance of observing
contractual obligations in one area of trade even when problems
were arising in another. The Chinese had hinted that their failure
to purchase U.S. grain reflected displeasure with the American
imposition of quotas on Chinese textile imports.

For the Chinese, the idea that law is separate from politics — an
absolutely indispensable precondition for trade in the West — is
a contradiction of Marxist-Leninist doctrine and thus particularly
difficult to swallow even when they understand the need to pay
lip service to it for foreign consumption. Due process is invariably
one of the keys to the preservation of the institutions of political

freedom. Yet even under authoritarian regimes there must, for business to operate normally, be a modicum of trust in the judiciary at least to handle commercial disputes legally and fairly. Time and again, American business executives, who frequently are lawyers, and, if not, take for granted the involvement of legal counsel in all major contracts, have been stunned by Chinese casualness toward law. "What protection or redress do I have if things go wrong with the deal?" an American executive is likely to ask. "You have our goodwill," a Chinese official is likely to reply with a smile. "You can trust the word of the Chinese people." Negotiating in China has reduced many strong men to tears.

Despite this, Peking has shown considerable sophistication in mobilizing its domestic talent and experience to make a highly impressive impact on the international commerce scene. No domestic Chinese organization exemplifies this better than one universally referred to inside and outside of China as CITIC, which stands for the China International Investment and Trust Corporation. A sort of Chinese government-owned investment bank, CITIC was founded in 1979 at the personal initiative of Deng Xiaoping, who promptly signed on savvy Shanghai businessman Rong Yiren to run it. Rong, seventy, a silver-haired survivor of Shanghai from the city's pre-1949 wheeler-dealer days, had the personal charisma, the confidence, and the drive to make end runs around China's cumbersome foreign trade bureaucracy to achieve his objectives. He also raided China's foreign ministry and other elite government units to recruit his personnel. Operating out of the corporation's sleek, bronze, twenty-nine–story tower in Peking (the capital's tallest building so far), Rong is one of a handful of Chinese with no Communist party status at all who is nonetheless able to get through to Deng Xiaoping directly on virtually any important project. Among CITIC's recent ventures involving U.S. exporters: the development of packaged food products with Beatrice and the sale throughout China of United Technology helicopters.

To a degree that would be unimaginable in any other Communist country, CITIC has won the respect and attention of top international financiers from many different continents. When the corporation celebrated its fifth anniversary in Peking in 1984, it invited bankers, top business executives, and economists from all over the world to an impressive seminar on China's trade and economy in Peking. That CITIC does not limit its energies to activities inside China affords an even more revealing insight into China's long-term notions of what Open Door may eventually mean. In May 1985, CITIC opened a four-member office in Manhattan's World Trade Center to deal directly with U.S. banks and corporations. Under Rong's able and sophisticated deputy Yao Wei, a former interpreter for Mao Zedong, it has been quietly investing directly in overseas factories, forests, and mineral resources. Incredibly, therefore, China's Open Door envisages something resembling a Chinese version of a multinational corporation. One of Rong's longer-range dreams for China: the establishment of a domestic Chinese stock market.

CITIC's success so far has largely depended on the personal drive and the connections of men like Rong Yiren and Yao Wei, both of whom received at least part of their education under Western auspices in Shanghai. When Rong and Yao move on, though, CITIC's best long-term hopes will rest on an entirely new generation of foreign-trained students, some of whom have already begun to return to China after years of studies in the West. In large measure, the continuity of China's Open Door policy as a whole, as well as the country's ability to keep up with developments in the rest of the advanced world, will also depend on new waves of "returned students," to use a phrase employed in the 1930s for foreign-trained intellectuals. An estimated 35,000 Chinese have gone abroad to study since 1979, and an astonishing 13,000 of these have come to the United States. Most have been graduate students or advanced research associates and have found their way into many of the prestigious American institutions of higher learning. Though a handful have defected to Taiwan or found a way of remaining in the United States, the vast majority will return.

With them, moreover, will come back into China more than just academic or technical qualifications. The cream of an entire gencration of Chinese brains will have been exposed to American freedom, American competition, American professional boister- ousness and vigor. It is inconceivable that the ideas and habits of mind they introduce into those circles of Chinese life to which they are reassigned on their return will not have a ripple effect, however slight at first, on the entire course of the country's future development, politically, culturally, and economically. If China continues on its present, moderate-reformist course, this devel- opment cannot help making China more open to international business and more conscious of international standards of law and commerce.

Yet CITIC and China's student population abroad are further indications, if any were needed, of the total seriousness with which Peking has chosen its current particular development road. In many ways, that intensity of purpose has thrown wrenches into the works of modernization even as it has speeded them along. Some of the more unexpected — and from the Chinese point of view disturbing — developments in the reform program have been cul- tural and social. The great leap that China's economy itself has taken has produced purely economic kinks and protrusions that have caused concern to China's leadership.

The most obvious problem has been the sheer overheating of the economy. In one of the most remarkable investment spurts of any large country in recent times, industrial growth in the first six months of 1985 hit 23 percent, instead of the planned 7 percent. A major factor in this was uncontrolled and unmonitored invest- ment by individual provinces and cities in projects neither ap- proved of, nor in some cases even known about, by the central government. In another interesting Chinese admission of economic difficulties, Vice-Premier Li Peng agreed that the 20 percent in- dustrial growth rate prevailing toward the end of 1985 was "much too fast." But he offered no suggestions on how to slow it down. For potential U.S. China traders, this apparent lack of control over investment should be a source of concern. It has already resulted in sudden and unannounced curtailments of foreign exchange availability as the central government has attempted to regain mastery of the national budget. Those curtailments, of course, have also affected foreign business opportunities in China. As China undertakes its slow but still remarkable self-transformation, Americans contemplating business in the People's Republic should insert this additional element of economic unpredictability into their calculations of risk and opportunity.

Neither Li nor, evidently, anyone in China's leadership has yet managed to find the key to allowing genuine economic decentralization while at the same time keeping a lid on overall growth. In many respects, the leadership has been learning as it has gone along. In November 1984, for example, the authorities naively announced that wage increases to be authorized in 1985 would be based upon rates prevailing at the end of 1984. The result: enterprises and collectives rushed to borrow money from the state banks to pad their payrolls. December bank loans amounted to a soaring 48.4 percent of all bank loans during 1984. To cope with the outflow of funds, as well as to finance import purchases greater than originally planned, Peking had to eat into $2.3 billion of its otherwise impressive foreign exchange reserves of $16.7 billion. At the same time, state and provincial foreign trading organizations suddenly found themselves strapped for funds to pay for goods already signed for. Several foreigners saw their deals float out the window on the winds of China's fiscal mismanagement. Others discovered that the money they had expected to be paid for items already delivered to the Chinese just wasn't there.

Assuming a continued rational leadership at the center of the Chinese administration, no domestic political crises, and no Chinese involvement in another military conflict, the People's Republic will most likely muddle through its economic problems. Foreigners will eventually get paid, capital growth will continue but with more careful controls, and the regime will discover some way to enable wages to reflect economic performance and prices to reflect real value. One aspect of China's modernization, after all, underlines China's earnestness about it almost as much as anything else. This is China's willingness to tie its growth to the engine of world trade.

Though at present international trade is still a relatively limited sector of the overall GNP of China, it is yearly assuming a higher and higher percentage of that figure.

Gradually, this is likely to lead to a point of no return for China's whole economic posture. Dr. Kenneth Lieberthal, professor of political science and research associate at the Center for Chinese Studies at the University of Michigan, comments: "What China is doing is making it possible that one of the two continental-sized Communist countries will join up with the international economy. If Deng's reforms work, therefore, he will have been the person to steer China toward the international economy and that will be the most significant international event of the 1980s. Over the long run, this may have a more profound effect than anything else he is doing." Lieberthal also points out a vital corollary of this in the event of severe slowdown in global and regional trade. "If you've got severe protectionism and a downturn in China's trade," he adds, "most of China's economic reform plans will have to be rethought." As Lieberthal readily admits, this is a high-risk approach to modernization. It is also one that puts considerable faith in the world marketplace as an efficient distributor of goods and services.

Foreigners for years have attempted to predict with assurance the development of things in China, and Sinology, both professional and amateur, is littered with discarded and discredited theories. The China trade is not for the timid, but it is similarly not for the impetuous. Just over the horizon lurk possible U.S.–China commercial contracts of gigantic proportions. If exporters of American nuclear technology were to overcome objections to its sale in China on both sides of the Pacific, for example, the total potential sales, according to some industry experts, could reach $8 billion, more than the entire two-way Sino-American trade volume at present. Yet American oil companies have already sunk huge amounts of exploration capital into so far dry holes in the South China Sea with no imminent prospect of eventual profit other than geological "probability" of the presence of oil. Trading with China

has always been something of a gamble. It will doubtless continue
to be so, with the exhilarating payoffs and gloomy losses characteristic of gambling never far away.

The very openness that has brought Chinese trade out into the
world scene, meanwhile, has been having side effects on Chinese
society that are proving risky for China, too, perhaps more risky
in the long run than China's current economic strategy. China in
the past has suffered internal turmoil from the dislocations to its
culture and polity engendered by too intense and too rapid exposure to the outside world. Some influences are more or less
predictable: crime, for example, or Western fashions in clothing
or music. Others, such as pressures for a politically more liberal
society, could prove more combustible within China than even the
farsighted Deng Xiaoping imagined when he acknowledged, back
in 1979, that opening China up would indeed bring in some "negative" influences. These developments should be of interest to U.S.
corporations looking into the China market, but they should not
divert American executives from a very obvious point: the United
States's trade with China, for all its kinks and oddities, has gathered
immense steam during the past decade. China's market potential
may not be unlimited, as incautious foreign observers have so often
imagined it to be ever since China first started seriously trading
with the West in the nineteenth century. But it is still huge. When
China's economic takeoff finally occurs, undoubtedly hastened
along by its foreign trade, Americans should not be mere spectators
of the event.

4

CHINA

Coping with ''Evil Winds''

THE VERY INTENSITY of China's recent opening up to the outside world has often exposed Deng Xiaoping to questions from both his countrymen and foreigners on the dangers to China of ideas and influences inimical to Marxist ideology. His answers have often been pithy and earthy. To a foreign visitor in October 1985, he declared: ''There are those who say we should not open our windows because open windows let in flies and other insects. They want the windows to stay closed, so we all expire from lack of air. But we say, 'Open the windows, breathe the fresh air, and at the same time fight the flies and insects.' ''

Deng was addressing, once again, the vexing question of how to deal with the angularities of opinion and sociology that have surfaced conspicuously in China ever since social and political restraints were gradually relaxed after 1979. Many of the things Deng had in mind are considered commonplace in other societies, including most of those of the Pacific Rim: pornography, prostitution, political unorthodoxy, to name the most obvious. For China, though, whose politics for thirty years has been totalitarian, the emergence of socially pluralistic tendencies, whether officially legal or otherwise, poses profound dilemmas. These are compounded by the ''theological'' tendency of Marxism-Leninism, especially in

China with its long history of ethical concerns, to blur the distinction between "sinners," understood ideologically as those opposed at heart to the regime and to Marxism-Leninism, and "criminals," who run the gamut from pickpockets to dissident poets.

In terms of what most people consider crimes in any society — theft, rape, murder, assault, and large-scale embezzlement of public funds — China experienced something of a crime wave during 1979–1983. Though the figures were still modest by the standards of many cities in advanced Western countries, street crime became a serious menace in many parts of China. Gang rapes and muggings were so common in Peking in 1982 and 1983, for example, that many people feared to be out in the streets at night in some parts of the city. The incidence of this particular sort of violent crime was nevertheless severely reduced by a brutal but effective anti-crime campaign that began in the late summer of 1983. All over China, thousands of criminals were humiliated in public by being paraded through the streets in open trucks, then executed by being shot in the back of the neck, in some cases, in public.

These harsh measures, which continued sporadically through much of 1984, sharply cut the rate of petty crime to the point where crime rates as a whole were down to 5.8 per 1,000 in 1984. By 1985 they had begun to edge up beyond 7 per 1,000, which was still below the 11 per 1,000 that they had reached in 1983. But the executions, and the lesser measures of sentencing to hard labor in the camps of Qinghai Province, China's equivalent of Siberia, failed to stop a new brand of crime in China: plain, old-fashioned, white-collar — or in this case, Mao-collar — corruption. The phenomenon, not new but vastly expanded in scope, has come to assume a prominence in the debate over the reforms as a whole that should be watched carefully by Americans and other foreigners. If China's leaders, for example, should feel that the cost in corruption resulting from the reforms is too high, they may be tempted to start closing the society down once again, preferring renewed economic decline to the manifestation of social tendencies they do not know how to control.

The Hainan Island car import operation was especially worrying to China's leadership because the scheme involved so many players in different walks of life at such a high level. The corruption had become almost "legal" by virtue of its sheer ubiquity. Yet other famous individual cases of Chinese corruption under the reforms have been hardly less dramatic. Liu Baoqin, for example, a minor official of Yutian County, outside Peking, came up with a scheme to defraud county officials and private individuals of a staggering $4.5 million in deposits for color TV sets he was supposedly planning to import from Hong Kong. When apprehended, Liu was living it up at a luxury resort hotel in Shenzhen, one of China's four Special Economic Zones, and in this case adjacent to Hong Kong.

That Liu was an official, however lowly, may have alarmed Peking authorities almost as much as the magnitude of his felonious activities. In September 1985, Politburo member Chen Yun, a close associate of Deng Xiaoping's during the early 1950s, but considered a critic of the speed of some of the reforms, complained that party and government officials and their children had managed to start up as many as 20,000 private businesses, "a considerable number of which," he complained, "collaborate with lawbreakers and unscrupulous foreign businessmen." In Shanghai, officials admitted that in the first seven months of 1985, 10 percent of all the crimes in the city were committed by party members, even though party members as a whole constitute a mere 4 percent of the total population of China.

For some Americans, starting up private business might seem a patriotic duty rather than a crime. But in China the very rapidity of the reforms, the blurring of distinctions between what is capitalist and what is socialist, as well as the complete reversal of old propaganda slogans, has seriously muddied the waters of what is and isn't legal. In addition, China has made a conscious effort to build up an operational legal system that can overrule local — and sometimes corrupt — Communist party officials, without conceding the principle that no one should be above the law. Part of the problem, too, is the uncertainty in the minds of China's own leaders as to what constitutes a "crime" or "corruption," and what constitutes the rather standard grease that makes the wheels of business turn in most Pacific Rim countries.

Several foreign corporations, for example, complain that it is often assumed that, in the wake of a major sales deal to China, the education of the son or daughter of the Chinese cadre overseeing the Chinese end of the deal will be paid for in the country of the foreign corporation. Other foreign firms resentfully admit that they often must pay for huge delegations of Chinese officials to go abroad on "inspection" or "training" visits to the corporation selling China the goods in question. Some foreign businessmen, particularly those based in Hong Kong, have at times been asked for 2 to 3 percent more than is standard in commissions, the extra to be paid into an account in a Hong Kong bank. Interestingly, most of those who have been the victims of such squeezes believe that the embezzlement on the Chinese side is corporate rather than individual, simply a way of providing the necessary slush funds for the business the Chinese unit is anxious to undertake. Corporate or otherwise, though, the issue raises very serious problems for American corporations, which have often had their fingers burned under U.S. law for wheel-greasing that is not prosecuted in Asia.

Unfortunately for everyone else, there have been persistent reports of Japanese companies' contributing to a free-for-all among Chinese officials by providing gifts to well-placed Chinese. In Canton, Japanese companies have been known to dispense VCR sets late at night to the homes of the officials who will make key purchasing decisions. Canton, by far the most foreign-influenced of Chinese cities since the 1979 reforms, is particularly corruptible because of the constant movement of overseas Chinese and foreign businessmen in and out of the city. A foreign hotel manager observed: "All the hotels here have problems with ladies of the night. It's coming back into fashion." Even in Peking, though prostitution has in general stayed away from the large hotels, which are often carefully watched by plainclothes police, it has surfaced informally on the fringes of the diplomatic community. Prostitution does not necessarily affect foreign business and international trade relations, of course, but its mere visibility in a society famed only a decade ago for its hostility to the mere mention of sex is indicative of how softened Chinese society has become in the past few years.

Chinese officialdom periodically denounces such phenomena in terms of varying vividness. Peng Zhen, chairman of the Standing Committee of the National People's Congress as well as a member of the five-man Standing Committee of the Politburo, has complained that "there are more sugar-coated bullets [of the bourgeoisie — a Leninist coinage] than ever before." The outraged Chen Yun has termed the new social developments "Eight New Evil Winds," a reference to a 1952 slogan used in a campaign against bribery, corruption, tax evasion, and other crimes against the newly installed Communist regime. Chen managed to include in his shopping list of newfound wickedness, however, such horrifying activities as the distribution of Western suits by some factories to their employees in lieu of an otherwise vetoed monetary bonus. "We must realize by opening up [to the outside world]," grumbled Chen, "that we cannot avoid an invasion of rotten capitalist ideas." Deng himself, never one to be careless of the direction of the prevailing political wind, has been no less reticent in attacking what he himself calls "the corrosive influence of capitalist ideas."

Yet between Deng's "corrosive influence" and Chen's "Eight New Evil Winds" there is a potential universe of difference. Deng and Chen, for example, probably agree on what constitutes pornography, and both almost certainly object to prostitution and the notion of Chinese women, even if not actually prostitutes, cohabiting from time to time with Western men. Each man, though, almost certainly differs on the much less concrete areas of Western ideas that are not inherently definable as "criminal." Chen, for example, lumped together in his 1985 criticisms "dirty newspapers, sex videos, and capitalist propaganda on capitalist liberty and democracy." Deng Xiaoping, naturally, is himself no closet liberal. Yet his own elevation to power as China's "paramount" leader was largely on the back of a widespread Chinese belief that he was indeed less oppressive and more democratic than other Chinese leaders. Calls for "capitalist liberty and democracy" were especially widespread during the ill-fated "Democracy Wall" movement in China of 1978–1979, a period of highly public free political expression through wall posters in the center of Peking. Deng is largely regarded as the principal force behind the unusual and extended police toleration of the movement.

He also seems far more realistic about the extent to which the "flies and insects" of a Chinese society with its windows open to the outside world can readily be eliminated from daily life. In his own tough and abrasive way, he gave his approval to the launching of an ominous campaign in the fall of 1983 against "spiritual pollution," a catchall phrase putatively directed against social decadence, but used by overzealous party cadres to designate virtually any and every Western influence, good, bad, or neutral. The social clampdown that came with the developing campaign embraced everything from theater to hairstyles, with petty government officials resorting to such inanities as ordering women to keep their long hair tied up in a bun or fastened at the back of the neck with a rubber band. The campaign even managed to lump together with pornography and decadence "religion," a domain of activity to which Peking had quietly sought to permit a measure of genuine autonomy in the late 1970s and early 1980s. Many of China's Protestant and Catholic Christians, who together may number as many as 50 million, feared a return to the repression of the Cultural Revolution years, when every single church in China was closed for nearly half a decade.

Many other ordinary Chinese began to worry that a renewal of the oppressive agenda of the Cultural Revolution itself was in the offing. A number of foreign business executives suddenly found that the Chinese officials with whom they had previously been on cordial and relaxed terms were no longer willing to associate with them, perhaps for fear of being subsequently charged with having consorted with "decadent" people. The entire episode was a sobering reminder to foreigners of just how fragile China's sense of ease in relation to the rest of the world really was — and may still be. With his characteristic pragmatism, Deng called off the campaign as soon as he saw the damage it was beginning to cause in the country.

Behind the vituperation against "spiritual pollution," however, lay an inherent Chinese ambivalence about the outside world that has manifested itself many times since the Jesuits first attained access to the Ming Dynasty court in the sixteenth century. Today, with China once again open to the outside world, such antiforeignism is clearly not in the ascendant. Yet it has certainly not disappeared. In early 1985 a violent riot at a soccer match in Peking revealed strong animosities toward foreigners when a Hong Kong soccer team defeated China's own players. After the game, many foreigners' cars were stoned. The anti-Japanese sentiments, though ostensibly the product of specific Japanese business practices in China, such as alleged dumping, are also useful reminders that China's exposure to modernization from foreign sources carries with it risks of sometimes violent reaction against the outside world.

Grass-roots "soccer violence" in China, along with remarks by men of Peng Zhen's stature about the "sugar-coated bullets" of alien ideas, reflects a genuine Chinese uncertainty about the value of foreign customs and ideas. For many conservative-minded, inherently Stalinist party stalwarts foreign things in general are symptomatic of a tendency toward political heterodoxy that has arisen with the loosening up of the old Maoist rigidity in Chinese society. In this domain there is no divergence of view between the Deng reformers and the Peng Zhen and Chen Yun centralizers. Both groups, along with the security authorities, are completely intolerant of any political ideas that contradict the orthodox Leninist view of Communist party supremacy over state and society. China's most prominent spokesman for political democracy and human rights, Wei Jingsheng, still languishes in prison, serving out the brutal fifteen-year sentence he was given for "espionage" in 1980. Wei's "crime" was to have told a foreign journalist the name of the Chinese military commander during the brief Sino-Vietnamese war of 1979. His real offense was to have made a case, eloquently, powerfully, and in public, for an extension of China's modernization to the sphere of domestic politics. The title of his most famous writing is "The Fifth Modernization: Democracy." Wei, with very little knowledge of how democracies actually work in the West, intuitively stumbled across the notion that a more open society must inevitably end up questioning the premises of political authoritarianism. He wanted to know why Chinese were not permitted to do this sort of questioning.

No Chinese leader ever really responded to Wei, at least not publicly. Instead, after the "Democracy Wall" movement had served its purpose of creating a temporary display of public opinion behind the move to reinstate Deng Xiaoping, it was brutally crushed by the security authorities. Yet among many Chinese intellectuals, there remains a powerful sympathy for the notion of political reform as a corollary of economic development. A graduate student at Fudan University, who said he himself was a party member, confided to a foreigner just before President Reagan addressed part of the student body in April 1984 that less than a fifth of Fudan students believed in Marxism. Another Fudan student late in 1985 told the same foreigner: "Economic reform will have to lead to political democratization. I have studied the Western countries and I can see that all of them have a much higher degree of democratization."

To an extent that would be unthinkable in the Soviet Union or much of Eastern Europe, in fact, Chinese students today openly voice their feelings about their country, about modernization, and about their aspirations for China. Many of their sentiments must be disquieting both to the security authorities, responsible for rooting out any incipient antiparty or antigovernment sentiments, and to China's own leaders. At the same time as the anti-Japanese wall-poster movement at Peking University in the fall of 1985, for example, there were other posters calling for constitutional changes to permit greater democracy. How deep or extensive such sentiments are in China's youthful student cadre is unclear. As long as China remains as open as it currently is to the outside world, however, and as long as the country continues to experience the rising expectations and the strains of a forced-pace modernization, it is unlikely that they will diminish in intensity. Among China's students in the United States, among newly returned young people, or even among thoughtful undergraduates at Chinese universities today, there could well be men and women stubbornly determined, sooner or later, to bring their aspirations for reform and greater political openness to bear upon a society less and less convinced of the efficacy of traditionalist Marxism-Leninism.

Some of these incipient feelings of alienation from Marxist-Leninist dogma have already been glimpsed among China's top leadership itself. In 1985, Deng Xiaoping made a joke to a visiting foreign delegation about his well-known deafness in his right ear that would have been unimaginable in any other Communist country that year. "Marx sits up in heaven," he said, "and is very powerful. He sees what we are doing and he doesn't like it, so he has punished me by making me deaf." The cheerful irreverence revealed not merely a contempt for Marxist economic dogma for its own sake but a colossal self-confidence about the path China itself has chosen. In an important way, if Deng can communicate his own self-confidence to his reform-minded successors-in-waiting and present colleagues, he will have gone an enormous distance toward lessening the difficulties of his own succession.

This is of no mere academic interest to American business executives and government analysts of the Chinese scene. One of the perennial worries of U.S. officials is whether Sino-American relations, today in relatively good order, can survive the political retirement or death of Deng Xiaoping. Those relations are inextricably linked with China's Open Door policy and the slow but unmistakable transformation of Chinese society itself. If, therefore, China's reforms were to falter with Deng's departure, the Peking-Washington relationship would likely suffer a perceptible cooling off, too. Unchecked, such a development would lead to a perceptible shift in the entire complex of Pacific Rim politics. In this event, not just U.S. trade and security interests with China but the entire American stake in the Pacific Rim would face new risks.

The uncertainty in Chinese political life is not a pleasant element for Pacific Rim neighbors of China, or traders with it, to have to face. But the fact that things can indeed go wrong in China is not a reason for assuming that they must do so. Perhaps the most remarkable achievement of Deng has been to portray consistently as "normal" a political and economic state of affairs that, by Chinese standards, is not so: namely, an orientation of openness and even candor toward the outside world. Interestingly, increasing numbers of Chinese do regard the reform era in Chinese life as "normal," rather than the previously "normal," but in fact politically volatile, era of Mao Zedong. This, in time, is likely to alter subtly but very positively China's climate of opinion toward the outside world in general and foreign trade in particular. There is thus still a good chance that things will go right in China. Even if the country is still far away from having any kind of mass consumer market, the trend toward greater trade and greater economic openness will reverberate throughout the country in ways that seem likely to strengthen China's current commercial links with the United States.

Deng himself has sought to heighten the optimism about China among foreigners by assiduously downplaying his own role and undercutting any tendency among those around him to develop a Deng personality cult. He has done so in such a way as to make it hard for like-minded Chinese reformers to duplicate his clear political preeminence. Speaking with an obvious sense of ease to a large American delegation in the Great Hall of the People in October 1985, Deng answered a specific question about his own place in history. "I don't want people to honor my memory," he insisted. "Never. Because I don't deserve that. Because what I do is nothing other than what reflects the wishes of the Chinese people and the Communist party members in China. . . . I was one of the principal leaders of China [before the Cultural Revolution] and I think that I should also be held responsible for the mistakes made during these years. I think there is simply no one, no one who is perfect. So that's why I never want to write a memoir. Never."

Leaving aside the self-protective reference to the "wishes of the Chinese people and the Communist party," Deng's self-deprecating comments reveal a modesty and sense of mortality that he has expressed over several years to many different people. Deng has, for example, spoken of "going to meet God," as Mao did, but

Deng's reference, in an interview in 1974, added the joking qualification that he was not sure whether his record would be ac-
ceptable in "the university of life." Many thoughtful scholars of
China believe such an ironic sense of self only fully emerged in
Deng during the Cultural Revolution, when his keen and broad-
ranging mind had ample opportunity to reflect on the odd vicissitudes of life, especially for people close to supreme national power.

For all of his irreverence toward Marx, Deng has made no such
slighting references toward Lenin. There is little doubt that Deng
is a convinced Leninist, a leader in whom the authoritarian instinct
is natural and unself-conscious. Interestingly, Soviet critics of China,
skeptical though they sometimes are about Deng's economic program, have never impugned his loyalty to the Leninist view of the
Communist party. This sense of Deng's fundamental commitment
to continuing Communist party control in China may well be the
key to his success in having pushed through controversial economic and even social programs without arousing uncontrollable
antagonism from political and ideological conservatives. In addition, of course, Deng has displayed an almost uncanny political
sense of when to bend to opposition and when to meet it head-
on and overcome it. Many Americans who might be tempted to
believe Deng is a "liberal," or that China is "going capitalist,"
should ponder this aspect of Deng's personality carefully. Deng
Xiaoping is a political authoritarian who regards Marxist-Leninist
terminology as a useful frame of reference to justify authoritarian
politics. He is also an economic goal-setter entirely unconvinced
by Marxist-Leninist economics. But he recognizes resistance to his
own economic policies when he sees it.

Much of such political opposition to Deng and China's present-
day reforms as has surfaced, has come, albeit obliquely, from men
of Deng's own generation who have worked with him politically
for four decades or more. Two of the most prominent are clearly
Peng Zhen, chairman of the Standing Committee of the National
People's Congress, and Chen Yun, First Secretary of the Central
Committee for Discipline Inspection — in effect, the party's "mor-
als police." Both men are members of the currently five-person

Standing Committee of the Politburo. Peng wields considerable influence in the National People's Congress, whose Standing Committee has the right to discuss party and government policies. At times, Peng has appeared to use the Standing Committee platform to question some of the Dengist reform policies. Deng's former Politburo colleague of the 1950s, though, former economic planner Chen Yun, eighty, has been a more powerful and effective spokesman for what may be a worried "conservative" faction in the Central Committee. Such a faction, presuming it exists in some form or other, does not necessarily disagree with the need for reform as such, only with the headlong pace with which Deng is conducting it. It is also clearly more disturbed, as we saw earlier, by the "flies and insects" that have blown in along with the other aspects of Western technology and skills.

Outside observers have always been hard put to identify exactly the nature of China's internal political debates, usually conducted in Aesopian language in different parts of China's official press. But close to the top of the list of continuing controversies is how large a role free market economics will play in China's development. For Deng, "there are no fundamental contradictions between the socialist system and the market economy." The only two cardinal principles of socialism in Deng's view, as he has told foreigners, are the dominant role of public ownership and the need to "try to avoid polarization [of wealth] . . . and to keep to the role of common prosperity." Chen, by contrast, offered a significantly more rigid definition of the relationship of the market to central planning during the Party Delegate Conference held in Peking in September 1985. "A planned economy," Chen carefully pronounced, "must remain as our primary goal; a market economy can only be a supplementary measure for temporary adjustment." Reminded by a foreign visitor that there was disquiet in some Chinese political circles over the course of the reforms, Deng did not directly demur. But he added: "Compared with what happened seven years ago, when the reforms first started in the countryside, the different views now are on a much smaller scale."

Deng has attempted to minimize those differences not just by installing prominently his own supporters at the highest and second-highest levels of the party and government, but by trying to lessen the degree of suspicion toward the reforms that clearly exists in the provincial and county-level party committees. At China's political center, loyal party General Secretary Hu Yaobang, sixty-eight, has a good chance of being succeeded by another Deng loyalist, Hu Qili, fifty-six. Similarly, Premier Zhao Ziyang's putative successor is Moscow-trained Vice-Premier Li Peng. (Li and Soviet leader Mikhail Gorbachev were acquaintances as students at Moscow University.) Even though the reformists have managed to install loyalists as party chiefs in almost all of the provinces (Hunan and Shandong are two prominent exceptions), they have made relatively little headway in the provincial party committees as a whole or in the even more rigid and intractable county party committees. Yet it will be at the grass roots in China's countryside and small country towns that the reformist program will — or perhaps will not — take solid root among the rank and file of Chinese Communist party officials.

In Shanghai, something of a testing ground for the success of Deng policies, the initial results are mixed in terms of China's overall reform, but solid as regards U.S. commercial relations with China. Some U.S. corporations have shown interest in Shanghai as the locale for joint venture and direct investment. The best known is Shanghai-Foxboro Ltd., a minority-investment subsidiary of the Foxboro Company, a Massachusetts-based manufacturer of precision instruments and machinery controls. The plant, which was operational in 1982 and was visited by President Reagan during his China trip, was already profitable in 1984. As is usually the case with joint ventures in China, the manager is Chinese and the deputy manager foreign, in this instance American. Several American businessmen visiting in the fall of 1985, however, were struck by the relatively low technological level of the production. Even though one-third of all the employees were graduate engineers, much of the equipment assembling and checking was done by hand at workbenches in a way many felt already obsolescent. Paradoxically, a more impressive example of Shanghai's role in the bandwagon of Chinese modernization was a factory in Hong-qiao Township, on Shanghai's outskirts, where textile workers fabricated men's clothing for Sears, Roebuck. Not everyone was impressed with the enterprise, however. Noticing the poor protection of the workers from the machinery, one American commented: "I think OSHA [the U.S. Occupational Safety and Health Administration] would close this place down."

Maybe it would, but that might be a shame for both America's China trade and China's own internal social and economic development. Regardless of problems of industrial safety that certainly plague some Chinese factories, China's success in competing with Taiwan and South Korea at the low end of the Pacific Rim textile market in the United States is impressive. It appears to have strengthened Chinese self-confidence about the country's capacity to compete in the world market, a fact that cannot fail to enhance the status of those elements of China's leadership which favor further development of the Open Door policy.

In contrast with Shanghai, Canton, 6.1 million strong, is a buzzing hive of entrepreneurial energy and drive. In the 1960s and 1970s, it was a sad, run-down city, its traditional ties to Hong Kong and the outside world cut off, its business-minded citizenry silent and resentful under the prevailing leftist ethos. Yet Canton was one of the first cities in China to take off commercially and economically as soon as the rural reforms became effective in 1979. The rich farmlands of the Pearl River delta and the energetic suburban peasants quickly transformed the city's food-supply scene, making it one of the best provided in all of China. In addition, the growing influx of Hong Kong Chinese visitors and investors touched off a mini-boom among street vendors in Canton itself. Roadside stalls selling fruit, clothing, transistor radios, and an assortment of bric-a-brac blossomed. By the early 1980s it was hard and at times impossible to tell the difference between visiting Hong Kong youths and Canton's own young people, at least in regard to dress and hairstyles. More important, Canton's familiarity to and with foreign businessmen made the process of starting up new enterprises and joint ventures far less of a novelty than it was in Shanghai.

Not surprisingly, therefore, among the earliest signs of the reform program was the quality of hotels. By 1984 there were three first-class, internationally managed hotels in Canton, the multistory White Swan, the China, and the Garden hotels. All three were joint-venture investment projects involving Hong Kong money, and all were predicated on a fast turnaround of investment. Canton is the twice-yearly venue of the Canton Trade Fair, to which thousands of foreign buyers and sellers come in the spring and the fall to purchase China's export commodities and offer their own wares for sale. With a chronic shortage of hotel rooms over the years and a generally low standard of accommodation and service in whatever Chinese hotels were available, the three internationally managed newcomers instantly filled a pressing need in the city as well as provided both Chinese and foreign investors with swift profits.

Canton, true to its traditional role as a geographical intermediary between the rest of China and the outside world, has paid little attention to attracting large foreign investment funds for high-technology industry. For one thing, that role is supposed to be played by the Shenzhen Special Economic Zone on the China–Hong Kong border eighty-three miles away by train to the south. For another, Canton's traditionally close ties with Hong Kong have led to a spillover into Guangdong Province of many of the light industries that have traditionally prospered in Hong Kong but whose profits have declined with the rise in Hong Kong's wages. In some cases, Hong Kong Chinese have entered into small- and medium-scale joint ventures with Chinese organizations belonging to Canton City or to Guangdong Province. In other cases, the Chinese themselves have attempted to establish light industrial, consumer-oriented enterprises whose products are closely tailored to export demand as well as to domestic Chinese demand.

A typical example of the combined domestic-foreign approach to light industrial manufacturing is the Bai Yun (White Cloud) Agricultural, Industrial, and Commercial Combine. Originally the Bai Yun Commune, the combine evolved into a full-scale commercial and industrial operation only when it set up five factories — for pharmaceuticals, radios, toys, machinery, and bean-curd drying — and was allowed to process foreign export goods for Hong Kong companies anxious for new manufacturing sources. That was in 1980. Today, in addition to producing, for example, the Moxing 3800 Deluxe radio and cassette recorder (price, $60), Bai Yun has a toy factory in which about 1,000 workers, almost entirely young and female, turn out Cabbage Patch Kids six days a week. The average monthly wage of these women, all in their late teens or early twenties, is some $20, considerably less than the retail price of the Cabbage Patch Kids in a New York department store.

One group of American business executives was surprised, on touring the radio factory, to see how primitive it appeared to be. Hardly any of the tasks, such as soldering or assembling, were automated, and the technology appeared antiquated by the standards of production in other parts of the Pacific Rim. Yet for Bai Yun's management and staff, the vast majority of whom would have been transplanting rice seedlings two decades ago, even six-day weeks of assembly-line monotony must surely have seemed an improvement. At least they now have cash and there are things to buy. In the Nanfang Department Store, for example, the biggest and best-organized store in Canton, the items for sale indicate a change in buying habits and capacities of Guangdong consumers that is scarcely less than revolutionary.

A decade ago, by contrast, little was available other than the dire necessities of Chinese life: thermos flasks, cotton coats, a few electric fans and bicycles, and a handful of domestically produced radios. Today, Marlboro cigarettes can be had for 86 cents a pack, bottles of Martell Medaillon VSOP Brandy for $27.20, and air conditioners for $1,666. Outside, the store's parking lot is crowded every day with Yamaha and Honda motorbikes. Canton's streets, meanwhile, are thick with small retail stores that are privately owned and run, peddling everything from oranges to pop music cassettes from Hong Kong. Several Americans familiar with Taiwan or Korea in the 1960s have commented on how similar the fastest-

developing parts of China today, that is, the south in general, are
to that epoch in those two countries.

China's new consumerism is more apparent in Canton than in
any other Chinese city except one: the urban center of the Shenzhen Special Economic Zone to the south. Established in 1979 by
special order of the State Council, along with three other similar
SEZs (Zhuhai and Shantou in Guangdong Province, and Xiamen
[Amoy] in Fujian Province), Shenzhen was intended to serve as
an entrepôt of foreign investment and technology transfer in the
opening up of China. By far the largest of the three zones, it
occupies an elongated swath of 126 square miles of southern
Guangdong directly adjacent to the point where Hong Kong's
Kowloon Peninsula borders the mainland.

By any reckoning, Shenzhen is the closest thing in China to a
boom town. When construction of huge infrastructure projects
finally got under way in 1980, the population of the previously
sleepy border area was a mere 30,000. Today, it is ten times that
much. The city-center of Shenzhen is a forest of cranes and soaring
high-rises, including a fifty-four-story international trade building
that is the tallest building in China. Close to the giant, and brand-
new, classical-style Chinese customs building that was built at the
border of Hong Kong are thickets of high-rise apartment buildings
identical in appearance to the thirty-story blocks that cluster together all over Hong Kong itself. The broad streets hold a mix of
Hong Kong day-trippers by the thousands, pilgrims to China's
commercial wonderland from the still austere interior of the country, and foreign tourists and business executives entering China
from Hong Kong. If it is hardly possible to distinguish Hong Kong
from local Chinese in Canton, it is not even worth attempting to
do so in Shenzhen. The girls are prettier and more sophisticated,
the boys bolder and more savvy, than anywhere else in China. A
story circulating throughout China in 1984 — and, true or not,
widely believed — tells of a group of Communist Civil War vet-
erans who visited Shenzhen and wept at what they found. "Is this
what we fought for?" they are said to have asked.

Ironically, they may well have unwittingly asked the correct question. Shenzhen has not lived up to the fond hopes of its originators, who admit that 90 percent of the $3 billion joint venture and investment project money so far committed to the zone has come from businessmen in Hong Kong and Macau. Investment by U.S., European, and Japanese high-technology companies has been disappointingly low to the Shenzhen authorities, who in turn have been criticized by China's central administration for spending more money than they should have to promote trade and tourism as opposed to industrial development.

Yet the very concept of Shenzhen, however flawed, is a bold one and an irrefutable sign of China's commitment to open itself up commercially to the outside world. The original theory behind its creation was that it and other Chinese coastal ports would be conduits into China's still backward interior for foreign technological, management, and financial resources. The original list of four SEZs was briefly expanded into a total of eighteen, all of the other fourteen being major Chinese coastal cities. At the height of Peking's support for the SEZs, Deng Xiaoping toured Shenzhen in January 1984 and declared: "The development and experience of Shenzhen have proved the correctness of the policy of establishing special economic zones."

By midsummer 1985, the political winds had changed direction and Deng's reformist colleagues appeared to be in temporary retreat over the SEZs. Part of the problem was the heavy toll on China's foreign exchange taken by Chinese ministries and provinces that had set up businesses in the zones which were not competitive internationally. Another awkward point for the original proponents of the SEZs was a 1984–1985 auditing of Chinese companies there that revealed some 20 percent of them had violated Chinese foreign exchange control regulations. Unwilling to be caught out on a limb, Deng himself had begun to reflect new uncertainties in his own public comments by late 1985. The Shenzhen Special Economic Zone, he said, was "an experiment," which "could fail. We hope it will succeed," he added, "but if it fails, we can draw lessons from it." In effect, Deng was merely taking care not to be caught out on a limb over the SEZs in case China's political conservatives sought to use Shenzhen's shortcomings as a stick with which to beat more important aspects of the entire reform program.

At a typical Shenzhen enterprise, the China Aero-Technology Shenzhen Trading and Industry Center (CASTIC), some of the reasons for Shenzhen's failure to attract high-level technology investment from abroad were apparent. CASTIC, itself a subsidiary of the China National Aero-Technology Import and Export Corporation, a state-run trading company, is an unwieldy conglomerate employing 3,000 people and manufacturing such an unlikely variety of goods as aluminum sheeting, watches, and toy plastic tanks for export to Europe and the United States. Though the quality of the products seemed adequate, the means of producing them would fail most U.S. and European inspection standards. American visitors to CASTIC's factories in October 1985 came across workers spray-painting plastic toy parts without protective breathing masks and working at metal lathes without protective goggles.

Shenzhen in many ways epitomizes the conundrum facing China in its rush to absorb foreign technology and experience. In the nineteenth century, a popular slogan among China's would-be reformers while the Qing Dynasty was still in power was "Western learning for practical application, Chinese learning for the essence of things." China's reformers then, as they do now, sought to apply foreign skills to the antiquated structures of China's society and polity like a lacquer coating on a bronze vase. They were unwilling to acknowledge at that time, as they are reluctant to admit now, that the skills of technology and management derive as much from the social mindset of a community as from any abstract principles.

Today, Chinese society is much less removed from the rest of the world than the Qing Empire was from the West in the 1890s. Peasants in Anhui Province, for example, can see nightly television news footage from Washington or Paris. Deng's belief that China

can be modernized without undermining the still Leninist and
totalitarian structure of Chinese politics is certainly an ambitious
gamble. Not just Americans, but everyone living in the Pacific Rim
community must hope that the gamble pays off and that China
continues to modernize itself without choking in the process on
too rapid an intake of foreign influences.

5

CHINA'S
PERIPHERY
Hong Kong and Taiwan

THE VIEW FROM THE PEAK is incomparable. The great harbor sweeps to the west and east between Victoria, the built-up urban center of Hong Kong Island, and the Kowloon Peninsula half a mile across the water. Skyscrapers cluster together along the harbor front of Hong Kong, blocking the view, even from far above, of much of the harborside activity. In all directions there is movement: freighters, lighters, ferries, pleasure junks, sailing junks, police boats, cabin cruisers and yachts, even helicopters buzzing the maritime traffic. We are looking at the world's third most important financial center, one of Asia's four Newly Industrialized Countries (NICs) and the tenth global trading partner of the United States. We are also looking at one of the world's oddest political anomalies. Technically a colony, Hong Kong is a city-and-hinterland of only just over 400 square miles with an influence on world economics equivalent to that of major capitalist trading powers. And it does so with the approval of China, its neighbor to the north, the world's most populous Communist state.

Looked at historically, Hong Kong has prospered in the interstices between the decline of a global empire, Great Britain, and the rise of the world's largest Marxist revolutionary state. The colony — or "territory," to use the term coyly preferred by British

officials in Hong Kong anxious not to offend Peking — has flourished despite the almost offensive difference between its own life-
style and that of the nation to which it has always belonged. It
has also unwittingly demonstrated that, given a pervasive philosophical ethic of hard work and self-restraint (the Confucian tradition in Hong Kong's case), the best government, as Jefferson
said, is often the least.

Whether the Chinese authorities in Peking ever grasped this
point during their long and often painful negotiations over the
future of the British colony remains in doubt. At ceremonies in
the Great Hall of the People in Peking in December 1984, Britain's
Prime Minister Margaret Thatcher was praised by Chinese Premier
Zhao Ziyang for her "farsightedness and statesmanship" in signing,
with Zhao, the final version of the Sino-British Joint Declaration
on Hong Kong. The agreement, which the British claim has the
status of an international treaty even though it is not called one,
defines the steps that will be taken up to and beyond the resumption of Chinese sovereignty and control over Hong Kong on
July 1, 1997. It is a long and detailed document. What it claims
to do is guarantee the minimum possible disruption of the economic and social life of Hong Kong — and hence, indirectly, of
the Pacific Rim community as a whole — during and beyond the
remaining interim period of British control and the assumption of
Chinese administration. By any reckoning, it is an ambitious and
unprecedented accord: the commitment of a Communist government to maintain under its own rule most of the principal ap-
purtenances of capitalism.

One of the great conundrums of Hong Kong's situation is that
its future depends on an arrangement that is without precedent in
the annals of diplomacy. No one knows what can be done for the
people of Hong Kong if Peking reneges on its commitment. The
Chinese themselves don't know whether their vision of a fundamentally capitalist society in the framework of a socialist state is
realistic. As for the British, there is little they will be able to do
but wring their hands if things go wrong. If they do, though, it
will, yet again, be more than just the Chinese government, the

people of Hong Kong, and the British who are affected. The Pacific Rim community as a whole will have to look once more to its internal cohesiveness.

The Sino-British Joint Declaration commits the Chinese to preserving not just key civil liberties when they take over control of Hong Kong, but forms of government and institutions experienced Hong Kong residents and British officials regard as having been instrumental in Hong Kong's phenomenal success as a society and an economy. The civil liberties include the obvious ones of speech, assembly, worship, the press, and travel. The institutions referred to in the Joint Declaration include the system of British common law and an independent judiciary, along with the freedom of the judiciary to appoint its own judges. The Joint Declaration also specifies Hong Kong's continuing right to take part as an autonomous entity in different international organizations in the spheres of trade and international transport and communications.

These detailed terms were included in the agreement almost entirely at British insistence, and many of them were hammered out only in the final few weeks of substantive negotiations. In and of themselves, the terms of the agreement can no more guarantee Hong Kong's survival under Chinese control as a prospering, free-enterprise member of the Pacific Rim community than possession of a list of the rules of tennis can guarantee success at Wimbledon. What the British achieved in a skillful display of rear-guard negotiating tactics was to put the reluctant Chinese authorities on record in a far more detailed and concrete manner than Peking originally desired. They knew that there would be no legal form of redress if Peking should backtrack on its commitments. But they believed that the Chinese might find the cost of failing to implement concrete and itemized diplomatic commitments too damaging to the national prestige to risk attempting.

Hong Kong's rise in prominence from a nineteenth-century malarial hideaway for Chinese pirates to a position of global financial prestige is a remarkable demonstration of one of the truths about the nature of the Pacific Rim in the world economic system: the region has consistently demonstrated that the possession of natural resources is far less important to economic success than human industry and favorable social and political conditions. When Hong Kong was ceded in perpetuity by the Qing Dynasty of China to the British in 1842 by the Treaty of Nanking, its new rulers saw it as a useful naval base at the mouth of the Pearl River and a potential clearinghouse for Britain's growing China trade. The potentiality of its also becoming a major manufacturing center could hardly have even been imagined at the time, since Britain itself was only just beginning its own industrialization.

In large measure, indeed, a commercial entrepôt was initially what it became, earning fortunes for the merchant princes ("taipans") who headed the British trading houses engaged in business along the China coast. Yet for most of its history, it was never anything else. Right up until the Japanese attack in December 1941, Hong Kong remained little more than a typical British colonial backwater with an excellent harbor and some good but narrowly focused business opportunities. In 1945, at the time of the Japanese surrender, the population of the city was a modest 750,000.

The transformation of Hong Kong from a colonial backwater into a major power in world trade took place during the 1950s and 1960s, when refugees from the newly installed Communist regime on the mainland of China — many of them from Shanghai — fled south with their entrepreneurial skills and energy, and in many cases their capital. To house and administer the influx of hundreds of thousands of the new arrivals, and to defuse any tendencies to explosive polarization between rich and poor, the British colonial authorities were forced to co-opt the most successful Chinese businessmen as, in effect, corulers. They listened carefully to their views on the nature and needs of Hong Kong's rapidly growing and developing society and, without ever conceding in public any constraints on their authority, in practice developed a unique system of government that might best be called "consensus colonialism." This, when added to the effectiveness of British law and favorable international circumstances for sustained economic development, created the conditions for both a socially vibrant, though fundamentally apolitical society, and stunning international commercial success.

The real test of Hong Kong's maturity as a society did not come until 1966–1967, when China was plunged into the turmoil of the Cultural Revolution. The resulting spillover of radicalism from Guangdong Province in the form of riots and bombings led to a crucial test of the loyalties of Hong Kong's mostly Chinese police force. Neither they nor the Hong Kong public as a whole wavered in continued support for the political status quo. More important, though, China's unwillingness to exploit the Hong Kong unrest further or to attempt an overturn of British rule demonstrated the enormous diplomatic and economic value that Hong Kong had acquired for China. Significantly, the far smaller and less important Portuguese colony of Macau, on the Pearl River estuary fifty minutes away from Hong Kong by modern jetfoil, capitulated without resistance to Red Guard radicalism at the same time that Hong Kong was firmly quelling its own unrest.

The nature of Hong Kong's contribution to China is worth spelling out. It has, over the years, provided up to 40 percent of the entire foreign exchange earnings of the People's Republic. During the two decades of U.S. attempts to isolate Peking from world commerce, Hong Kong served as an essential, politically neutral staging-post for the transshipment of Chinese goods to the rest of the world. At the same time, Hong Kong provided China with a quiet but effective window on the West even at the very height of Cultural Revolution xenophobia and anti-Westernism during the 1960s.

Hong Kong became even more valuable when China began to open up to the outside world, first tentatively during the early 1970s, and then decisively under the reformist Open Door policies of Deng Xiaoping since 1979. At this point, the colony came into its own as a major commercial outlet for China itself. Hong Kong middlemen, skillfully exploiting their unique familiarity with both Chinese ways and Western commercial manners, brought Western technological and economic resources into contact with a Peking bureaucracy anxious to acquire them, but not always certain how best to do so. In 1985, Hong Kong's two-way trade with China amounted to $9.6 billion, surpassing that of China with the United States.

There are important reasons why Hong Kong flourished as vigorously as it did on the periphery of China itself, factors that help explain some of the most important dynamics of relationships within the Pacific Rim community. One ingredient was the British understanding of China's need not to "lose face" in Hong Kong. With exquisite precision, British governors and officials showed meticulous respect for Chinese nationalistic and cultural sensibilities. The acts they performed may seem trivial and silly to many Americans: dotting the eye on the dragon figurehead of boats paddled in the annual Dragon Boat Races (the one who makes the final dot is believed to obtain good luck); punctiliously attending China's annual October 1 National Day celebrations in Hong Kong; bowing solemnly to a photograph of Mao Zedong in the Bank of China after the chairman's death in 1976. The British severely curtailed the activities of political groups in Hong Kong, forbidding them to organize anti-Communist propaganda and cracking down on any Hong Kong–based subversion or sabotage efforts directed against the mainland. All of these efforts were accepted by Peking as a sort of unstated "psychological tribute" that Britain was paying for its continued occupation of Chinese territory.

Chinese "face" was preserved in another important way. The Hong Kong branch of Xinhua News Agency, the official news outlet of the People's Republic, was allowed by the British to evolve into a de facto representative office of the Peking government. The leaders of other Peking front organizations in Hong Kong, such as the Bank of China or China Resources, though without any official diplomatic status, were also treated with a deference normally due the nominated plenipotentiaries of a major state. In return for such evident lack of challenge to Chinese feelings about Hong Kong's ultimate sovereignty, Peking's appointed Communist representatives in Hong Kong kept the colony's leftist labor unions docile and unconfrontational. They also did not publicly challenge Britain's administrative prerogatives.

If all of Hong Kong's 412 square miles had come under the original Treaty of Nanking cession by China, this remarkable balance among conflicting interests might have taken a prosperous Hong Kong into the twenty-first century unruffled. Almost certainly, Peking would have preferred this. It would have been content to live perhaps indefinitely with the ambiguity of Hong Kong's colonial status as long as the British did not flaunt their rule and did not claim that Hong Kong had ceased to be part of China. Unfortunately, this was not possible. The New Territories, by far the largest single portion of Hong Kong land area, had been ceded to Britain not in 1842, but in 1898, under treaty terms that explicitly expired after ninety-nine years: June 30, 1997. What propelled Margaret Thatcher's Conservative government in 1982 to clarify the issue of Hong Kong's post-1997 status was something important, though quite mundane: the status of fifteen-year mortgages and loans whose maturity would occur after 1997.

Thatcher's first official visit to Peking in September 1982 was breezily hoped by the British to bring about an uncomplicated Sino-British agreement on Hong Kong that in effect would prolong indefinitely the status quo. Instead, it led to months of bitter wrangling over the sovereignty issue, with the British trying to use their own concession on this matter as a lever to secure Chinese acquiescence in the continuation of the British administration. It was an issue the British could not win, but in the course of the arguments between the two sides, what was laid bare high in Chinese officialdom was an astonishing and disturbing ignorance of how capitalist societies work. British negotiators told friends that they were appalled at how uncomprehending their Chinese interlocutors were of the most basic characteristics of a capitalist economy, such as the relationship of currency exchange rates to trade performance, interest rates, and the status of international stock markets. One irritated British official commented about his Chinese opposite numbers during the talks, "What do they understand of capitalism? Has any of them ever lived in a capitalist country?"

In an explanation of the nature of the Sino-British Joint Declaration to visiting Americans, Hong Kong's Governor Sir Edward Youde, a former British diplomat with ten years' service in China, described it as "an internationally binding form of an agreement to maintain in Hong Kong a free enterprise, capitalist economy open to the rest of the world." Youde acknowledged that there was "no policeman in the last resort" if China failed to live up to its commitments in dealing with the colony after Britain had officially withdrawn from it.

In a separate address to the U.S. business group, China's unofficial "ambassador" to Hong Kong, Director of the Xinhua News Agency Xu Jiatun, appeared at first merely to echo this position. "The Chinese government," he said, repeating precisely the official Chinese position on Hong Kong, "settles the question of Hong Kong on the concept 'one country, two systems,' with the aim of recovering the sovereignty over and maintaining the stability and prosperity of Hong Kong. To this end, the Chinese government has laid down that the existing capitalist system of Hong Kong will remain unchanged for fifty years after 1997." Xu added: "It is our sincere wish to maintain the capitalist system in Hong Kong. This is a long-term strategic policy formulated on the basis of various factors."

Xu's placatory comments were in line with articles in the Joint Declaration that commit China to creating a new status for Hong Kong as a Special Administrative Region, under which the governor will be "elected" by "the people of Hong Kong," but subject to approval by China's State Council. The definition of this SAR is then supposed to be clarified by the codification of a new basic law to be included in China's constitution. So far, Peking has not made it at all clear that the kind of electing it has in mind will not differ greatly from Communist elections anywhere else. In practice, China would evidently like to take over the pre–Joint Declaration British colonial structure of government in Hong Kong, in which politics has played virtually no role at all and such elections as have occurred have been for positions on low-level "district boards."

But by 1997, if the current experiments with democracy being attempted by the Hong Kong government continue, that Hong Kong will have already vanished.

The British began extending electoral positions among Hong Kong's "district boards" in 1979. More recently, in September 1985, twenty-four "novices" — a term designating a new category of member — were elected by limited-qualification "functional constituency" groups to the 56-seat Legislative Council, a hitherto appointive organ with purely consultative functions. The indirect elections for a legislature are part of a tentative British program to encourage the growth of genuine representative institutions in Hong Kong as fast as they can take root. According to Governor Youde, such developments have been "quite irrespective of the 1997 negotiations." According to Xinhua's Xu Jiatun, however, "to turn the Hong Kong administration over to the Hong Kong people in the next twelve years is contrary to the spirit of the Joint Declaration." Xu merely promised, without elaboration, that China would give "a high degree of autonomy" to the people of Hong Kong after 1997.

The difference in approach between Governor Youde and Xu Jiatun is not just a matter of taste in the nuances of diplomatese. It represents the crux of the problem of Hong Kong's transition to Chinese rule and illustrates how uncertain Hong Kong's future after 1997 still is, in spite of the Joint Declaration. Such deliberately vague but high-sounding declarations as those uttered by Xu were pronounced repeatedly by China during the tough and often bitter negotiations between Britain and China during the interval from Thatcher's visit in 1982 and her signing of the Joint Declaration in December 1984. They were accompanied, on Peking's part, by an often vituperative propaganda assault on the British negotiating position and by thinly veiled threats that China would impose its own solution if the negotiations were not concluded satisfactorily within a two-year timetable. This Chinese war of nerves provoked a bad case of fright in the colony's financial markets, especially during "Black November" 1983, when the stock market's Hang Seng index fell below 1,000 for the first time since 1976 and the

Hong Kong dollar plunged from $5.4 to one U.S. dollar at the start of the talks to $9.75. An estimated $1.3 billion in private capital meanwhile fled Hong Kong for safer havens overseas.

Eventually, enough trusted Hong Kong Chinese supporters of the People's Republic made their voices heard for China to back away from the strident rhetoric, which was seriously damaging, among other things, the property values of Chinese-owned real estate in Hong Kong. Ironically, some of Peking's measures intended to restore confidence in Hong Kong — including a massive injection of investment capital — had the opposite effect from what was intended, giving some Hong Kong residents the impression that Peking was attempting to exert its influence in Hong Kong long before 1997. Other propitiatory signals also backfired. To placate just one of the more concrete fears, Chinese officials informally revealed that they did not plan to do away with Hong Kong's horse racing, a highly popular pastime with both the rich and the poor of the colony. Yet when Peking declared that Hong Kong's social customs would be "basically unchanged" after 1997, speculation was as wide as the Pacific over precisely where Peking would get tough and where it would be tolerant.

The Joint Declaration and the warm words by China at the signing helped soothe some of the nerves in the British colony, providing at least a grain of hope, that, against all precedent, Hong Kong under Chinese rule would continue to exist on China's southern periphery as a boisterous, independent-minded capitalist enclave with a distinctly unsocialist life-style. Despite the public display of assurance, however, many British officials remained chagrined by their experience at the negotiations. Businessmen in Hong Kong took a cautious approach. While not accepting at face value China's reiterated assurances that it would indeed "preserve" Hong Kong, they did not come to the opposite conclusion that all was not lost in the territory from the perspective of economic opportunity.

By late 1985, the uncertainties of the whole 1997 issue seemed in Hong Kong to have been forgotten for the short term. Between then and 1997 there were, after all, at least two five-year periods, the generally agreed quick turnaround time for investments to show profits in many sectors of the economy. The property market had revived, moreover, after its doldrums during the negotiations, and foreign capital continued to be invested. For the colony's well-educated and able Chinese middle class, though, such evidence of economic buoyancy was unlikely to still the considerable doubts many felt. Many still continue to feel them, doubtful that Peking can avoid smothering Hong Kong as an economic and social entity after 1997. Prime Minister Thatcher acknowledged as much in Peking in 1984, when she admitted that the people of Hong Kong had "expressed some reservations" about the agreement.

For those with the financial resources and the connections, there has been and remains the possibility of quietly obtaining foreign citizenship. During 1983–1984, in fact, numerous Hong Kong professionals were comparing notes on which of a series of countries (Fiji, the Philippines, Portugal, the Dominican Republic, Paraguay, Thailand, among others) offered the best deal for a passport on the basis of a minimal economic investment (reportedly as high as $200,000 in some cases and as low as $5,000 in others). The humor of such passport-shopping aside, Hong Kong would be but a shadow of its former self if a substantial portion of its Chinese senior management and professional cadre opted not to stay when British rule ceased.

For Americans, this is not just an academic issue. The U.S. stake in Hong Kong is considerable. Total U.S. investment is estimated at $4 to $5 billion; 14,000 Americans live in the colony. In addition to being Hong Kong's preeminent trading partner, only recently rivaled by China, the United States is particularly well represented commercially. An estimated 800 U.S. firms operate in Hong Kong, including IBM, Westinghouse, Exxon, and Texas Instruments, and have large corporate establishments in the colony. Several U.S. corporations use Hong Kong as a regional base for operations throughout Asia. U.S. exporters have done well in Hong Kong, selling electronic components, semiconductors, business machines, and vegetables and fruit. With a per capita GDP of $6,090 in 1985, and living standards the second or third highest in Asia behind

Japan and possibly Singapore, Hong Kong has become a heavy purchaser of U.S. consumer goods, importing more American goods per capita ($577) than any of the Pacific Rim countries and more even than the European Economic Community. Finally, Hong Kong has long served the United States as a politically safe and popular port of call for ships of the Seventh Fleet.

The prominence of American business in Hong Kong and its actual growth there since the signing of the Sino-British accords reflect two of the positive things about the British colony in the face of disquieting possibilities. First, the city is probably the most dynamic example of untrammeled free enterprise in the world. Second, most of Hong Kong's Chinese today are not acting as though they were about to face doom in the immediate future. Hong Kong, as the late Australian journalist Richard Hughes observed in a book on the colony, has been living on "borrowed time." The five-year turnaround schedules for new investments are standard projections. Many of Hong Kong's Chinese live as though there were no point in planning for tomorrow. Yet, paradoxically, this "invest-now, profit-now" philosophy is what has made Hong Kong such a massive financial and manufacturing success. The city's dynamism, its excellent communications, and its splendid location — on the belly of China and within arm's reach of the rest of Southeast Asia — have made it a magnet for U.S. corporations seeking strong and semipermanent regional headquarters in Asia.

The enormous U.S. stake in Hong Kong has been a major factor in Hong Kong's economic dynamism and self-confidence. By the same token, any hint of a change in U.S. trading policies causes great anxiety in the colony's governing circles. Hong Kong's trade officials argue that were the Textile and Apparel Trade Enforcement Bill — from Hong Kong's point of view, the most threatening of the protectionist bills proposed in the U.S. Congress — enacted into law, it would increase prices for textiles in the United States by 10 to 30 percent. They also note that the bill would ride roughshod over a series of bilateral agreements painstakingly worked out over a long period of time. Speaking to American executives,

Governor Youde devoted a major part of a long address to the dangers of protectionism to Hong Kong and, he claimed, to the United States itself. "It is for this reason," Youde said, "that Hong Kong views with alarm any trend towards protectionism, especially in the United States. Hong Kong knows well that open markets and fair trading practices are the only sound basis for the healthy development of world trade. What is more, we practice what we preach. Our domestic market is probably the most open in the world." Hong Kong, in fact, is the one member of the Pacific Rim community that has been even more open to U.S. goods than the United States has been to goods from the rest of the Pacific Rim. It is thus by far the least "deserving" of any protectionist measures by the United States.

The United States cannot remain indifferent to Hong Kong's evolution in the years leading up to the Chinese takeover in 1997. It must also pay special attention to what happens in the immediate aftermath of the British departure. During the Sino-British talks, American officials either maintained a discreet silence or else they talked bullishly about the territory. Yet U.S. analysts know that the Chinese approach to Hong Kong will provide important clues to the likely behavior of the People's Republic toward the other, politically far more significant entity on the rim of China, namely, Taiwan. A satisfactory solution to the continuing political enmity between the People's Republic of China and the Republic of China government on Taiwan would remove a major element of geo-political uncertainty from the entire Pacific Rim. By contrast, a wrong move by Peking or a domestic political crisis in Taiwan that prompted intervention from the mainland could, just as seriously as a new Korean conflict, be an important setback to all of the region's great promise. In many respects, China's takeover of Hong Kong could be a "dress rehearsal," for better or for worse, of what it would do in Taiwan after reunification with the mainland had taken place.

Meanwhile, American business, taking its cue from the attitudes of Hong Kong's Chinese themselves, is booming in Hong Kong as though the territory's current status were guaranteed forever. It is not, of course. It is simply that American business has discovered that to act as though it were is probably the best way of restraining China from attempting anything now or immediately after 1997 that will upset the profitability of Hong Kong.

By promising, and after 1997 even practicing, "leniency" toward Hong Kong, Chinese officials are clearly making a bigger pitch for cooperation by Taiwan in a similar solution to the question of Taiwan's reunification with the mainland. "The reunification of Taiwan can be achieved on the basis of the Hong Kong formula," Xu Jiatun explained, "and our policy would be even more generous." By that he was referring to Peking's offer to Taiwan to keep its own armed forces and for Taiwan's current leadership to have a role in the central government of the People's Republic itself. Peking's current policy toward Taiwan is to offer a peaceful process of reunification after mutual talks, with full guarantees for the preservation of Taiwan's current economic and social system. The ongoing peace offensive was initiated by a nine-point letter in 1981 from Chinese Politburo member Marshal Ye Jianying to Taiwan's president Chiang Ching-kuo, son of the late Generalissimo Chiang Kai-shek. The focus of Peking's current wooing of Taiwan is clear. It is to persuade not just Taiwan's leadership and people, but also the outside world, especially the United States, that nothing but stubbornness on the part of the Kuomintang leadership of Taiwan is preventing a final, peaceful conclusion of China's six-decade-old civil war.

At the time of the U.S. opening to China under President Nixon in 1972, Chairman Mao Zedong himself expansively suggested that there was no urgency to reunite Taiwan with the "motherland." The process, he and other Chinese leaders indicated, might take fifty or a hundred years to complete. Unquestionably, such an ambling timetable helped persuade the United States that Peking was no longer interested in any solution to the Taiwan issue but a peaceful one. Yet, annoyingly for many American policy-makers anxious to allay fears among Taiwan's supporters in the United States, China refused explicitly to rule out the use of force against Taiwan. Chinese explanations that such a pronouncement would amount to a limitation of national sovereignty were accepted at face value by U.S. diplomats.

Despite China's "peace offensive" of the early 1980s toward Taiwan, however, evidence has never been far from the surface that China's leadership is not as patient about solving the question as Mao himself indicated. In September 1982, the Twelfth Congress of the Chinese Communist party, with Deng in the ascendant, designated Taiwan reunification as one of the three outstanding party tasks of the 1980s. Chinese officials later explained that the party call had been intended as a guideline, not a deadline. More revealingly, China's impulsive Communist party General Secretary Hu Yaobang made it apparent in May 1985 that the use of force was still very much under consideration in Peking's ongoing assessment of how to deal with Taiwan. Speaking to Lu Keng, director of the Hong Kong–based newspaper *Pai Hsing*, Hu explained the circumstances for use of force: "If the broad masses of the Chinese people wish to return [to the mainland] and a small number do not wish to return, it will be necessary to use force." Hu admitted to Lu that he did not think most people on Taiwan wanted reunification with the mainland at this point, but he suggested that those in favor of the change would grow in numbers year by year.

Hu's hypothetical scenario has to be taken seriously by the United States and other Pacific Rim contingency planners, if only because Peking has never felt squeamish either about using force against recalcitrant regions of China or about asserting that those regions' "broad masses" fully supported such a move as "liberation." With remarkable, but for Hu quite typical, candor, the Chinese party leader went on to say that China would be in a position to modernize its defense sufficiently for such an attack upon Taiwan in "seven, eight, or ten years." He also reinforced an indirect threat that Deng Xiaoping had made with visiting Japanese politicians, to the effect that China might consider enforcing a blockade if Taiwan absolutely refused to enter into talks with the mainland. Hu explained, "If we have the strength to enforce a blockade and if Taiwan vehemently opposes reunification, we shall have to consider enforcing a blockade." In the long, highly detailed interview, Hu added that China would not attempt either a blockade or an assault upon Taiwan unless it were sure of success under all circumstances, including possible intervention by the United States.

In the Department of State in Washington, this sort of talk tends to be airily dismissed as too unlikely a scenario to merit much thought. Assessing Hu's words, one official said that, should Peking use force, the United States "would reconsider [its] policy of nonintervention." It would, in fact, have to do considerably more than "reconsider." Under the terms of the Taiwan Relations Act of 1979, both the President and the Congress are legally bound to take "appropriate action" in the event of a People's Republic attack upon Taiwan. Even though there might well be strong domestic inhibitions against an actual U.S. military intervention in East Asia on behalf of Taiwan, a contingency U.S. military response to a Chinese attack across the ninety-mile straits certainly cannot be ruled out. As is the case in the Korean peninsula, the assurance of a U.S. military response to aggression is more likely to prevent such aggression from happening than silence is.

Whatever some U.S. officials think about Hu Yaobang's musings, Taiwan's leaders take them seriously, as well they should. Referring directly to Hu's interview, Taiwan's Premier Yu Kuo-hwa told the Newstour, "As we see it, the threat of the use of force against Taiwan is an established policy of the Chinese Communist regime and they haven't done it yet because they are not fully prepared."

One reason for that — apart from Peking's obvious preference to use any means other than force to achieve reunification — is Taiwan's considerable self-defense capability. Some 40 percent of Taiwan's budget is spent on defense. Its well-trained and well-equipped armed forces of 484,000 could not defeat a truly determined invasion attempt from the mainland, but they serve to render such an attempt too costly to undertake at present. Taiwan's air force of U.S.–designed, but Taiwan-built F-5 jets, along with superior morale and pilot training, has ensured Taiwanese air superiority over the Taiwan Straits. Taiwan is nevertheless under considerable pressure to develop its own advanced defense industry as rapidly as possible. The reason is Peking's successful diplomatic effort, under the terms of the Sino-American Joint Communiqué of August 17, 1982, to force Washington progressively to reduce each year the volume of arms it sells to Taiwan. The existence of the August 17 Communiqué, among other things, has so far inhibited even the relatively pro-Taiwan Reagan administration from agreeing to sell to Taiwan advanced new U.S. fighters such as the FX or the F-20 Tigershark.

Mindful of less than sterling support by the United States of other Asian allies in the past, Taiwan has prudently gone full speed ahead on its own high-technology military aviation program. It has already designed, built, and flown a high-performance jet trainer, the AT-3, which could be converted with little difficulty to a ground-attack role. What Taiwan seriously needs, though, is an advanced, second-generation fighter. It is already building such a plane, with an anticipated performance greater than Mach 2 (making it comparable, say, to the Israeli Kfir fighter). The aircraft will be powered by two U.S.–made Garrett engines. It is expected to make its first flight in 1987 and to be in service in the early 1990s.

Taiwan's ability to design and manufacture a high-performance jet fighter is a remarkable achievement for a country of 19.4 million crammed onto a heavily mountainous island the size of Maryland and Delaware combined. It reflects on two characteristics of the Kuomintang party that has ruled the island province since its defeat in 1949 at the hands of the Chinese Communists. One is the considerable skill with which the KMT has governed Taiwan. The other is the impressive level of popular support for the government in the face of international isolation, diplomatic rebuff by former allies, and military threat ninety miles away.

The emergence of the KMT as one of the most stable and effective ruling political parties in the Pacific Rim could not have been predicted by anyone three and a half decades ago. When the defeated and discredited troops and supporters of Chiang Kai-shek poured across the Taiwan Strait in 1949, the ousted Nationalist regime had become a byword for incompetence and corruption. To add to this legacy, the brutal suppression by mainland administrators of Taiwan's own provincial political aspirations in the late 1940s had created a wall of bitterness between the approximately one million Nationalists from the mainland and the estimated 10 million native Taiwanese. Today, though, in what observers regard as fair and honest elections for the National Assembly and various Taiwanese provincial assemblies, the KMT consistently obtains a solid 70 percent of the vote. In addition, though there is still a strong sentiment among many Taiwanese for an independent Taiwan that has cast off all political connections to the mainland now and in the future, intermarriage and a common educational system have narrowed the gap between the 15 percent mainland-originated minority and the 85 percent Taiwanese. Some 55 percent of voters in provincial elections report having relatives married to members of other provincial groups.

Taiwan's economic performance during three decades is well enough known not to require elaborate description. The salient points are simple. A per capita income of $110 in 1952 had become one of more than $3,000 by the end of 1985, surpassing that of the mainland by a factor of 12. An effective land reform program in the 1950s all but eliminated rural destitution, increased agricultural output, and has made possible a national primary school attendance statistic of 99.8 percent. When competitive exporting policies rather than those of income substitution prevailed in the 1970s, economic growth began to surge. From 1970 to 1984, annual growth exceeded 9 percent. It dropped to an estimated 4.2 percent during 1985, largely because of the slowdown in U.S. demand. Still, with the 1984 two-way trade figure amounting to $52.4 million, Taiwan was fifteenth among the world's trading nations and the fifth largest global trading partner of the United States.

Even more remarkably, Taiwan's phenomenal development surge was not accompanied by the widening income gaps common in so many developing countries. While the richest 20 percent of Taiwan's population in 1952 had an income 15 times that of the poorest, by 1982 that had dropped to 4.29 to 1 and was still falling. Today, more than 50 percent of Taiwan's adult population identifies itself as middle class. Inflation was regarded by many as the chief economic factor behind the downfall of the Nationalists in the late 1940s on the mainland. Today, at 0.5 percent for 1985, Taiwan has one of the lowest rates in the world.

The record is not all pristine. Taiwan was shaken in February 1985, for example, by the financial collapse of the Tenth Credit Co-operative and the Cathay Investment and Trust Company. The companies, two of Taiwan's largest private financial institutions, went down amid charges of shady business practices and political cronyism. Overall, though, Taiwan's economic rise in less than four decades from Third World indigence and backwardness to the front ranks of world trading nations, without the emergence of serious inequities, and while bearing a huge burden of defense expenditure, ought to be given due credit. Taiwan for several decades has simply been one of the best-governed less-developed countries in the world.

This, along with a universal and genuine distaste for Communism in the population as a whole, has contributed to a wide measure of popular support for the KMT regime. The KMT is certainly not democratic in the American sense of the word. There are no opposition parties permitted, and martial law, in effect since 1940, provides the authorities with sweeping powers to arrest and imprison political opponents on charges of subversion. There have been abuses of this system and civil rights violations. From the U.S. point of view, by far the most egregious was the murder of the Chinese-American Henry Liu in San Francisco in October 1984. Liu was killed as a consequence of an unseemly collaboration between Taiwan's Bamboo Union gang and the chief of Taiwan's military intelligence, Major General Wang Hsi-ling. Wang and two subordinates, whose connection with the murder was uncovered by an independent Taiwan government investigation, were arrested and sentenced to life imprisonment, though it is still unclear what the motive for the murder was.

The striking thing about the Liu murder was how out of character it was with a regime that has done everything possible in recent years to become politically more open and to avoid the charge of arbitrariness. Taiwan, while strongly authoritarian, is not totalitarian in the Communist party or Nazi party sense. There are opposition representatives in the National Assembly and Legislative Yuan, under the revealing label of Tangwai (literally, "outside the party"). Taiwan's press is largely free to write what it wants about the government, provided it does not openly advocate either accommodation with Peking or independence for Taiwan. There is complete freedom of choice of employment, of movement, of marriage partner, of religious worship and proselytization (or lack of it), and substantial, though not complete, freedom to travel abroad. All of these areas of activity are severely restricted in China. There is also a steady opening up of the channels of public discussion. Most interestingly, when critical commentary arose late in 1985 in the Taiwanese press about members of the family of President Chiang Ching-kuo, Chiang himself argued against a crackdown on the criticism by the authorities.

For many Americans, this might seem all rather trivial. For the residents of an island lacking any democratic traditions (Taiwan was annexed by Japan in 1895, when the Qing dynasty was still ruling China, and ruled by them until 1945) that by the skin of its teeth avoided Communist takeover in 1950 and thereafter such disasters as the Great Leap Forward and the Cultural Revolution, it is a lot to be thankful for. The ultimate point for most Taiwanese is that their fellow Chinese on the mainland all along not only endured far worse economic conditions than they did, but had to put up with tyranny along with poverty.

American foreign policy officials anxious for freedom of diplomatic movement with the People's Republic of China have tended to look upon Taiwan as an annoying encumbrance. There it is, uncompromisingly insisting on its official title — the Republic of China — and obstinately claiming to speak for the whole mainland. Its very existence is a reminder of U.S. foreign policy in a different age, of support for the losing Nationalists in the war with the Communists four decades ago. Its leaders and representatives, though unfailingly polite, are to many Americans like embarrassing images of their own past, of the uncompromising American anti-

Communism of the 1940s and 1950s, and of the strong bonds of sympathy that Americans used to feel for the beleaguered regime of Generalissimo Chiang Kai-shek. (Chiang's American-educated wife, Mei-ling, from 1943 to 1967 appeared every year on the list of the ten women in the world most admired by Americans.) To add to the problem, China's own diplomats play endlessly on American support for Taiwan, suggesting to them that if only this last remnant of misguided foreign policy were removed, nothing would stand in the way of complete harmony between Peking and Washington.

Yet Taiwan, not unlike Hong Kong or South Korea, has thrived economically and socially while confronting a major, even if not always an imminent, risk of takeover by a politically hostile regime. It is a testimony of the character of Chinese living on the island and yet another example of the strength of mind and purpose that has made the Pacific Rim what it is today. The U.S. business community on the island is particularly admiring of Taiwan's achievements and vigorously pursues every possible development of the U.S.–Taiwan trade relationship.

It would certainly be imprudent for the United States to yield to Chinese pressure on Taiwan, either by leaning on Taipei to negotiate with Peking, or by attempting to undo the considerable ties that Taiwan maintains with the United States. Two-way U.S.–Taiwan trade in 1984 alone was $19.8 billion, more than three times the U.S.–China trade that year. There are also far more substantial airline and sea links with Taiwan than there are with the People's Republic. It is true that the United States has had a number of problems with Taiwan in the trade area, such as protectionist tariffs on imported cars and other items, and pirating (though by now much reduced from before). Yet Taiwan's overall commercial and business climate is still far more congenial to U.S. interests than that in the People's Republic. And in light of Peking's past history of domestic political uncertainty, it is still likely to remain so in the future.

There are also important strategic reasons why the United States should be in no hurry to see Taiwan come under the control of

Peking. Though they are too discreet to mention this publicly, the strongest supporters of continued non-Communist rule on Taiwan are the Japanese, who were, interestingly enough, the first to employ the term "unsinkable aircraft carrier" for the island. Taiwan sits astride all of Japan's major trade arteries with Southeast Asia, the Middle East, and Europe. Even though the People's Republic is not now actively hostile toward Japan, the Japanese are more conscious of the size and potential military power of China than most Americans are.

So far, at least during the Reagan administration, Washington has shown a fundamentally sensible approach to the China-Taiwan issue, neither needlessly antagonizing Peking with largely rhetorical gestures to Taiwan (i.e., by upgrading the nonofficial quasi-embassy on Taiwan, the American Institute in Taiwan, to official status), nor caving in to it by refusing to nominate for air routes to China U.S. carriers concurrently serving Taiwan. At the same time, Washington has firmly resisted Peking's efforts to ask for a repeal of the Taiwan Relations Act. The act correctly states that any Peking threat to Taiwan "is of grave concern to the United States." The act naturally sounds offensive to a China that believes national unification surpasses in importance all other criteria, including the actual desires of 19 million people and regional stability. But the act nevertheless serves as a useful reminder both that long-term alliances are not to be broken without good cause and that the future disposition of Taiwan is central to U.S. views of its interests in the Pacific Rim. Beyond that, if Taiwan's population should change its mind and show overwhelming interest in being reunited with the mainland on Peking's terms, no U.S. administration should stand in the way.

With or without the Taiwan Relations Act, it remains in the U.S. interest to discourage further erosion of Taipei's strained diplomatic situation. Only twenty-four countries still maintain diplomatic relations with the Republic of China as a sovereign entity, and one-third of these are tiny island-states in the Pacific or the Caribbean. In East Asia, only South Korea maintains diplomatic ties, and Seoul would abandon Taipei tomorrow if Peking agreed to exchange embassies with it. The most important of Taipei's diplomatic links are with South Africa and Saudi Arabia, from which it acquires the bulk of the oil it imports to satisfy 90 percent of its energy needs.

Taiwan has nevertheless been successful in establishing non-diplomatic but "substantive" ties with 126 areas and countries. Such ties include the United States's American Institute in Taiwan, Japan's Interchange Association, and the "Spanish Chamber of Commerce." Though these subterfuge embassies and consulates fool no one — for Taipei makes no attempt to conceal the fact that they are nothing less than quasi-official agencies of the governments — they are important. They enable Taiwan to carry on in legal fashion the international business and communications vital to its trade and indeed to its survival as an independent political entity. Their opposite numbers overseas, such as the Co-Ordination Council for North American Affairs, Taiwan's "embassy" in Washington, are no less essential both as substantive quasi-diplomatic links and as symbols of continuing political credibility. The United States could usefully contribute to the balance of power in East Asia by setting an example in its own handling of such "non-diplomatic" relations with Taiwan and by quietly encouraging other host countries to deal seriously with Taipei as an important commercial and political entity.

A continuing show of American interest in Taiwan's stability and prosperity is more likely than anything else to contribute to a satisfactory solution to the four-decade standoff between the mainland and Taiwan. It is not out of the question that a future generation of leaders on Taiwan will see advantages in reunification with a China that is, say, unmistakably headed in the direction of political and economic pluralism. Though Taiwan's demands that China abandon the "Four Principles" of its constitution (adherence to the socialist road, the People's Democratic Dictatorship, the leading role of the Communist party, Marxism-Leninism and Mao Zedong thought) are not realistic today, they could, presumably, be modified in time. Thus the United States should not seek, as it has often been tempted to in other parts of the world (in Nicaragua or Iran, for example), a radical change of political power within Taiwan for the sake of a supposedly more rapid movement toward Chinese reunification.

For one thing, 85 percent of the population of Taiwan is Taiwanese. The overwhelming majority of these people would not want to overthrow the KMT if this weakened Taiwan's overall state structure vis-à-vis the Communists. Independence for Taiwan, if truly feasible, might or might not be a good thing for the Taiwanese under a benign climate of diplomacy on the Pacific Rim. At this point, though, the slightest indication of a political move by the government in Taipei in that direction would do more than anything else to trigger off a military assault by the mainland. It is in the United States's best interest to encourage Taiwan's KMT leadership to bring forward its outstanding talent and to institutionalize the smoothest possible form of political succession. Currently, there is no clear successor to the ailing President Chiang Ching-kuo, who will be eighty when his current term expires in 1990. One strong possibility to succeed him is Vice-President Lee Teng-hui, who is sixty-two and who would be the first Taiwanese president of the Republic of China.

It remains an intriguing fact of life in the Pacific Rim community that two of the major trading power components of it thrive in a state of political limbo. That limbo has at least been rendered less uncertain in Hong Kong's case: there is an implicit understanding between Great Britain and China that the existing social and economic structure has been an essential ingredient in Hong Kong's success. Taiwan, by contrast, has survived solely because it has not been militarily possible or diplomatically prudent for the People's Republic to attempt to take it back by force.

Neither of these situations is an entirely comfortable one to live with for the Pacific Rim community as a whole and for the United States in particular. Yet both illustrate the degree of maturity and resilience of two of the key Pacific Rim societies. They also demonstrate just how faithful, consciously or not, the rulers of these two countries have been to American concepts of free enterprise. With no sense of external security to rely on, Hong Kong and

Taiwanese entrepreneurs have built up dynamic and powerful economies that have motivated the people working within them to think beyond mere economics. Americans have repeatedly benefited from these trade impulses, as the continuing U.S. involvement in both Hong Kong and Taiwan makes apparent. The cases of Hong Kong and Taiwan fly in the face of the desire of a majority of political analysts for neat and decisive political solutions to complex problems. In each of these two societies, politics has taken a firm back seat to economics. That may have postponed important political decisions to just another day. But it has also demonstrated to the Pacific Rim the formidable resilience of commercial man under pressure from noneconomic quarters.

6

THE PHILIPPINES
Democracy's Return

THE END OF THE MARCOS ERA came with a suddenness that hardly anyone would have predicted even a few weeks earlier. Tired, unable to walk unaided, and looking bewildered and subdued, the sixty-eight-year-old president of the Philippines found himself hobbling out of a U.S. Air Force transport plane onto the tarmac of Hickam Field in Honolulu. It was February 26, 1986, and only hours after he had ordered himself inaugurated president in an almost comic-opera ceremony at the luxurious Malacañang Palace in Manila. As presidential guards anxiously kept watch over all approaches to the palace, a hand-picked audience provided the necessary backdrop of enthusiasm and support. They applauded him, smiled, and allowed him to believe that a handful of loyalists, at least, had still not accepted that the twenty-year era was finally over.

In some ways, for Ferdinand Marcos and his family, it was not over at all. As the days at the V.I.P. guest quarters at Hickam Field turned into weeks, attention in the United States turned increasingly to the considerable wealth that Marcos had brought with him aboard the two U.S. aircraft used to transport his entourage from Clark Air Base in the Philippines. The estimated one million dollars in pesos, the hundreds of thousands of dollars in gold bullion, and the perhaps millions of dollars' worth of diamonds and other precious stones were one thing. No less important were documents that appeared to link Marcos to an estimated $5 to $10 billion that he and his family, by some allegations, had milked from the Philippine economy and spirited out of the country into safe havens around the world. There was little likelihood that Marcos himself would be extradited from the United States back to Manila, whatever his possible wrongdoings. Newly inaugurated President Corazon Aquino had already ruled this out. What did seem possible was a long, and for the United States embarrassing, wrangle over how to weigh the legitimate needs of privacy for the exiled Marcos family on the one hand against clear American obligations to the new Philippine government on the other. If billions of dollars had in fact been skimmed off the Philippine economy for personal use by the ousted regime, then clearly Washington was honor-bound to help Manila recover it.

The awkwardness over the Marcos wealth was, and is, an emblem of the highly unusual relationship forged during a relatively short time between the United States and the heterogeneous Philippine archipelago of 7,100 islands in the South China Sea. It would not be accurate to call the relationship one of love and hate. Love and suspicion would be closer to reality, even though vituperative Filipino anti-Americanism has become, as in many Third World countries, a staple for a small segment of the alienated leftist intelligentsia. The very first emotion felt toward the Americans by most Filipinos was the elation and gratitude of 1898, when the United States was instrumental in bringing more than 300 years of Spanish colonial rule to an abrupt end. Then that feeling was tempered with disappointment and resentment as U.S. "liberation" turned into a new colonial rule by Americans, indeed, the unique example of direct colonial rule in the history of the United States.

Still, the American administration of the Philippines during the brief half-century 1898–1946 was on the whole remarkably benevolent. A touching paternalistic affection for Filipinos on the part of many Americans led, for example, to efforts at raising educational standards in the islands as a whole unmatched by any other colonial administration. Today, despite the deplorable state of its economy, the Philippines has more people in college-level education than any other country in Asia (including Japan). The 1981 figure was 26 percent, a percentage higher even than the U.K.'s (20 percent) and Switzerland's (18 percent). From early on, the United States also made it clear that its colonial rule would be limited in time. In 1934, it initiated steps for eventual complete independence of the Philippines, a move that undoubtedly contributed to the heroic resistance of Filipinos to the Japanese occupation. During World War II, the Philippines was one of the few Japanese-occupied countries in South and East Asia with a truly effective indigenous resistance movement. When the Americans returned in 1944, they were greeted as genuine "liberators" from the Japanese in a manner completely different from the resentful acceptance by the Vietnamese of the French return to Indochina or the British return to Burma at the end of World War II.

The United States kept its word on independence for the Philippines in 1946, bringing into existence the first full-fledged ex-colonial democracy in Asia. Americans themselves were popular and warmly received throughout the country. Even today, in the provinces, small boys tend to welcome any white-skinned person with the cheerful "Hi, Joe!" — a throwback to the days when the only Americans seen were U.S. soldiers, i.e., G.I. Joes. With large numbers of better-off Filipinos coming to the United States for higher education, with the widespread acceptance of the English language (today the second official language of the country after Pilipino), with American culture becoming familiar throughout the country, it was not always easy to know when U.S. interests ended and Philippine interests began.

Two of the greatest benefits to the United States of the warm and informal friendship between it and the Philippines were the 99-year lease agreements on Subic Bay Naval Base and Clark Air Base. For the first three decades or so of the original 1947 Military Bases Agreement there was little friction between Washington and Manila on the mutual benefit of the bases or the best mutual terms

for their continuation. The warm pro–U.S. world view of all of
the post-independence Philippine governments assumed a natural
commonality of security interests between Washington and Manila
in the western Pacific. In the context of the U.S. policy of "con-
tainment" of Soviet and Chinese Communism during the 1950s,
most Filipinos regarded the presence on their territory of the largest
U.S. naval base and the largest U.S. air base outside of American
soil as highly desirable. It was thus natural that when the Southeast
Asia Treaty Organization was formed in 1954 to combat Communist expansionism in Malaya, Indochina, and the Philippines,
the implementing treaty should have been signed in Manila in
1954.

That treaty itself grew out of a determined and successful effort
by the Philippines to rid itself of a dangerous and fast-growing
Communist movement, the so-called Hukbalahap revolt that broke
out in 1950. In one of the first and most successful counterinsurgency campaigns in modern history, a popular and energetic
Philippine secretary of defense, Ramón Magsaysay, defeated the
revolt by a skillful blend of grass-roots reforms, amnesty for returning guerrillas, and vigorous military leadership. For Washington, Magsaysay was the model of the nationalist, anti-Communist
developing-country politician, an incorruptible and charismatic figure
at odds with both leftist insurgency and the venality of the wealthy
landowning classes that had helped foment it. By 1953, the Huk
rebellion had been broken and Magsaysay had been propelled by
his own success into the presidency of the Philippines. Warmly
supported by Washington, though opposed by Philippine legislators who saw his proposed reforms as a threat to their vested
interests, Magsaysay did his best in his four years in office to
translate Philippine democracy from a debating society for the rich
to an instrument for political participation by all Filipinos.

Magsaysay died in a plane crash in 1957, beloved by his countrymen and deeply mourned by them. Until the accession of Corazon Aquino, there died with him the best U.S. hopes for preventing
the decay of Filipino society into widening income disparities,
unchecked corruption, and local political gangsterism. Political de-

mocracy continued to function in the Philippines into the late fifties and sixties, but it became more and more a way of resolving baronial disputes between squabbling members of the wealthy oligarchy. From time to time, candidates for the presidency campaigned on platforms of "reform" and opposition to the visible corruption of the incumbent regime. Ferdinand Marcos himself came into power with a broad popular mandate in 1965 as a wartime anti-Japanese guerrilla leader eager to galvanize the stagnant economy, improve rural conditions, and implement educational reform. When he was reelected in 1969, he was widely regarded as having succeeded in many of these objectives. He was the first Philippine president since independence in 1946 to be reelected to a second term in office.

In its alliance with the Philippines, the United States was largely, though not entirely, hostage to the abilities and reputation of whoever was in office as president of the Philippines at the time. In 1970 and 1971, in particular, Washington was especially beholden to Marcos as a firm and supportive Asian ally at a time when U.S. policy in Vietnam was under attack both at home and around the world. In terms of his alliance with the United States, Marcos certainly "delivered." He had sent a 2,000-man engineer unit to South Vietnam at the request of President Johnson in 1966, and he made no objections to the U.S. use of Clark and Subic Bay as key staging bases in the war effort against North Vietnam. In the early 1970s Marcos paid for that assistance to Washington with increasingly violent, leftist-led anti-American and anti-Marcos demonstrations in his own country. The failure of his administration to keep up with the expectations of better life in the countryside, along with an evident increase in the corruption of his regime, obviously contributed to the rising radicalism of political opposition elements, especially in Manila. Few Americans in 1971 or 1972, though, would have argued with the obligation of Washington to do what it could to enable the Marcos regime to succeed in the Philippines. In addition, the alternatives to Marcos in 1972 did not, in American eyes, look any more appealing as leaders of the Philippines than Marcos himself did.

Ever since Spanish times, political violence was close to the surface of Philippine life, especially under the quasi-feudal order of things in the provinces. Nor did it vanish after independence in 1946 and the advent of constitutional rule, but took its victims both inside politics and out of it, revealing even in presidential elections the deep passions of personal vendettas and political jealousies. With the rise of street demonstrations against the Marcos government and the United States in the late sixties, political manners declined further. By 1971, Manila was one of the most dangerous cities in Asia, with popular nightclubs typically asking patrons to check their firearms at the entrance.

Marcos tested the waters of international, and particularly U.S., opinion in August 1971, when he temporarily suspended habeas corpus in the wake of a brutal terrorist grenade attack during a Philippine election campaign rally in Manila's Plaza Miranda. In retrospect, this action, the precipitating event for which was suspected by many to have been a "terrorist" action staged by the Marcos regime itself, was a dress rehearsal for the following year. When, on September 21, 1972, Marcos had his Secretary of Defense Juan Ponce Enrile impose martial law on the entire country, the action had been well prepared and the pretexts set forth with legalistic precision. The country, Marcos alleged, was undergoing challenges to its very survival as a society, with a three-fold assault upon legitimate government: a Communist insurgency in northern Luzon led by the New People's Army, a dangerous Muslim secessionist movement in Mindanao and the Sulu Islands, and a breakdown of law and order in the streets of the nation's cities.

Marcos's assertions about the collapse of national security would have been more convincing if he had not moved immediately to arrest leading political opposition figures, notably Benigno Aquino, leader of the Liberal party. Aquino and several other political associates were rounded up in the predawn hours by military police and taken into detention at army camps around Manila. But the most significant impact of martial law upon ordinary Filipinos was the imposition of a curfew from midnight to 5:00 A.M. and a severe crackdown on street crime. There was thus a noticeable improvement in what the regime called the "peace and order" situation. For urban dwellers in particular, many of whose lives were untouched by the coming and going of democratic political life, martial law seemed at first to offer a real improvement in the quality of life. If there had been a genuinely free plebiscite on martial law in the early and mid-1970s, Marcos would very probably have won it.

It is easy today to blame successive U.S. administrations for allegedly unthinking support of the status quo in the Philippines during the twenty-year Marcos era. The fact is, Marcos was both effective and popular during his first decade in power, regardless of the dubious legality of his actions or his darker motives for staying in power. Particularly after the traumas of violent anti-American demonstrations in Manila in 1971 and 1972, life for the 50,000 or so Americans living in the Philippines improved dramatically in the first years of martial law. Indicative of the overwhelming approval for the Marcos move by the American community at the time was a congratulatory message sent to Malacañang Palace by the American Chamber of Commerce in the Philippines in 1972. "The American Chamber of Commerce," the message went, "wishes you every success in your endeavor to restore peace and order, business confidence, economic growth and well-being of the Filipino people and nation. We assure you of our confidence and co-operation in achieving these objectives."

With the benefit of hindsight, it is easy to see that Marcos had a mixture of motives throughout his personal and political life. During World War II he was neither the spotless guerrilla hero of his own political image-makers nor the cowardly collaborator of the Japanese depicted by his political opponents. When he declared martial law, he obviously was worried about the greatest combination of internal threats to the security of the Philippines since independence. At the same time, he wanted to stay in power at all costs and knew that the political winds by late 1972 were swinging strongly against him. The national emergency was a convenient reason not to have to step down from office.

Marcos often told visitors to Malacañang Palace in the seventies that he was concerned about his role in history. With his considerable intelligence he cast around for some sort of philosophical peg upon which to hang the new political order he was building up under martial law. He came up with the slogan "constitutional authoritarianism." For the sort of Philippines he said he wanted to create with his new powers, he coined the term "The New Society." He even claimed to have rediscovered the original, pre-Spanish Malay roots of the Filipino polity, the *barangay*, a term that may loosely be translated as "village community." Marcos's first attempts to legitimize martial law electorally were barangay elections. He appeared for a while to have revolutionary intentions for his country. The barangays, and later the creation of a prime minister's office and a National Assembly, were a conscious effort to prevent people from thinking in terms of the old politics, which, however corrupt, was at least free.

But Marcos in his last decade as president became ill. He suffered from lupus erythematosus, a disease of the skin that, in its systemic form, as appears to be the case with Marcos, affects such organs as the kidneys. It was particularly ironic for a man who, during the 1970s when he was in his mid-fifties, was exercising strenuously up to three, sometimes four, hours a day every day of the week (his main activities: weight lifting, waterskiing, pelota, and golf). Presumably, the illness had some effect upon his overall political judgment. Even if it did not, personal greed and the corruption inevitable with too much power for too long, did. Marcos did not seem able to control, in particular, the frenetic and spend-thrift activities of his wife, Imelda, whose appetite for political power and international social recognition diluted the otherwise serious tone of government Marcos always tried hard to project from his paneled office in Malacañang. Ultimately, surrounded by flatterers, cronies, and opportunists, Marcos lost even the ability to distinguish between genuine ability and eager sycophancy, and, as it related to the state of the nation as a whole, between desirability and actuality. In the end, this more than anything sealed his fate with the United States. Washington might have been willing to countenance an autocrat who was corrupt but effective, but not one who was corrupt, inffective, and singularly out of touch with what was happening in his country.

For masses of ordinary Filipinos, though, Marcos lost whatever last shreds of respectability he had still maintained with the murder of opposition political leader Benigno Aquino in August 1983. The only man in the Philippines with intelligence and political skills equal to those of Marcos himself, Aquino from the early 1970s onward was the one serious obstacle to almost indefinite presidential power for Marcos.

Aquino's meteoric rise to national prominence began early. At only nineteen, he was an acclaimed and decorated war correspondent for a Filipino newspaper covering the Korean War. At twenty-two, he was elected governor of Tarlac Province, the youngest man ever elected provincial governor in the Philippines. By his early thirties, Aquino had been elected senator and emerged as leader of the Liberal party. A man of immense energy and considerable rhetorical skills, Aquino — or "Ninoy" as he was invariably called by his admirers — alone had the personal charisma and political intelligence to challenge Marcos for the presidency of the Philippines. By the early 1970s, he had not only emerged as the Liberal party's chosen champion against Marcos in the general elections scheduled for 1973, but also was clearly the one opposition politician most likely to vanquish the politically canny Philippine president.

After martial law in 1972, Aquino spent seven and a half years as a political prisoner in the Philippines. During this time Marcos devoted a large amount of his own legal and propagandistic ingenuity in attempts to destroy Aquino's political credibility and future with an assortment of complicated judicial proceedings. While in prison, Aquino obviously matured in both his political and his philosophical thinking. Filipinos and foreigners who were in contact with him at the time or later, when he was in the United States, said that he had undergone a Christian born-again experience in prison. This, he recalled in the United States, had drained from him the hatred he had long felt for Marcos.

In 1977, still held in Fort Bonifacio, outside Manila, Aquino was tried for sedition and sentenced to death. Thanks to protests from around the world, the sentence was never carried out and Aquino even ran for the National Assembly from his jail cell. His wife, Corazon, in her first direct taste of political action on her own, handled the details of the campaign, which was not successful. Three years later, in 1980, Aquino was permitted to leave the Philippines for heart surgery at Baylor University in Texas. He then settled in Boston for three years, lecturing at Harvard and M.I.T. While he was out of the country, Marcos dusted off the original murder conviction against Aquino and sentenced him to death in absentia on the original trumped-up murder charges.

Aquino had been repeatedly warned by Marcos representatives, including Imelda Marcos herself on a visit to the United States in the 1980s, that if he returned to the Philippines it might prove impossible to protect him from assassination. The warning was crudely cynical: only Marcos himself had profound, long-term interests in eliminating Aquino from the Philippine political scene. In the event, Aquino's murder, as he was led down the steps from a China Airlines 767 at Manila International Airport, was so clumsily staged as a "Communist" action that Marcos, assuming he personally knew of its planning and permitted it to go ahead, brought ultimate political disgrace down upon his own head.

Specifically, the August 1983 murder is regarded by most observers of the Philippines as the single political event that precipitated the collapse of the Philippine economy and the beginning of the end of Marcos's rule in the Philippines. After nationwide protests against the Aquino murder, Marcos was forced to establish an independent judicial commission to investigate it. The commission was to find in a majority vote that the Philippine military had carried out the murder, with responsibility proceeding all the way to General Fabian Ver, Marcos's first cousin and chief of staff of the Philippine armed forces. Ver was later formally charged and tried, along with more than twenty other military officers and enlisted men. He took a leave of absence from the armed services while the trial was under way. Late in 1985, he was found not guilty and for a brief period of time reinstated by Marcos in all of his official military positions. Even though he was to flee the country in February 1986 along with the Marcos entourage, there were early indications from the new Aquino government that sufficient new evidence might be forthcoming for the Aquino murder trial to be reopened.

The murder of Aquino revealed not just an evil core within the Marcos administration in the Philippines, but an uncharacteristic ineptitude. But it was the outrage aroused by the murder that provoked a large chunk of the Philippine middle class, as well as leftist students and others, to demonstrate publicly against Marcos. The "Yellow Revolution," or "People Power" revolt, of Corazon Aquino in February 1986 was in essence a middle-class revolution, a conservative revolution of people raised amid Christian ethics who were truly offended by the crude public trampling of them by the Marcos regime. (The term "Yellow" derived from the yellow ribbons that appeared around Manila in August 1983, when Aquino was due to return from his exile in the United States. After his assassination, yellow became the adoptive symbol of those wishing to commemorate Aquino and of opposition to Marcos.)

In the Philippines, as elsewhere in the non-Communist world, the middle class also means the business community. Most if not all Filipino businessmen not intimately connected with the Marcos regime were outraged by the Aquino murder. All, without exception, became first alarmed, then angered when the entire Philippine economy went into a nosedive as national and international confidence in the Marcos regime foundered. Business leaders and the Roman Catholic Church finally turned on Marcos, whose greed and arbitrariness damaged and offended both communities. Despite his control of the military and his supreme political instincts and skills, not even Marcos could in the end cope with this combination arrayed against him.

From early on after the Aquino assassination, large numbers of business leaders were publicly demonstrating against Marcos. Perhaps just as important, most of them were speaking unfavorably of the regime to outsiders. A respected Philippine economist, Bernardo M. Villegas, senior vice-president of the Center for Research and Communication in Manila, for example, put it this way to U.S. business leaders who visited the Philippines in early November. "The glib rationalization of President Ferdinand Marcos," he asserted, "cannot hide the fact that the Philippines is the economic basket case of Pacific Asia in 1985."

Villegas was not exaggerating. Only Bangladesh, in all of Asia, had a poorer economic performance record during 1983–1985. Yet not even Bangladesh had a total GNP decline of nearly 10 percent in the years 1984–1985. For the Philippines this was just one of the indices of economic woe. The others were hardly less alarming. Inflation was more than 20 percent for 1985, the peso had declined in value from 9 cents in 1983 to 5 cents early in 1986, and foreign indebtedness was estimated at $27.5 billion. To keep pace with this debt, the Philippines was forced to set aside $1.7 billion annually in interest payments alone, approximately one-third of its entire annual foreign exchange earnings.

At the microeconomic level, as Filipino businessmen were certainly aware, life for ordinary Filipinos in the last years of Marcos was as close to desperate as it had probably ever been since the end of the Japanese occupation. The per capita income at the end of 1985 was just $600 a year, a decline in real terms to the level of 1972, ironically enough, the first year of Marcos's martial law rule. A large majority of Filipinos had to get by on approximately $55 a month, with the poorest of them, farm workers, receiving wages of less than $2 a day. In the 21-million-person work force, underemployment was estimated at 40 percent.

The economic situation for ordinary Filipinos during the early 1980s was so bleak that only three factors of Philippine national life kept many in the countryside, where 80 percent of the country's 56 million people live, from actual starvation. One was the still-strong extended family system. Somehow, villages in the provinces always seemed willing to absorb family members suffering greater economic hardship than they themselves were. A second was an underground economy of barter and unreported retail sales that helped take up the slack of the decline of the monetary economy. A third was the estimated $2 billion annually remitted home to the Philippines by an estimated 2 million Filipinos working overseas. Despite these safety nets, malnutrition has stalked many areas of the Philippines for a decade or more, and it has clearly grown into a serious menace in those parts of the country worst hit by recessions.

Not all of the Philippines' economic ills are attributable to Marcos. The decline in sugar prices, for example, to approximately 5 cents a pound, has hit every sugar exporter in the world. Serious drops in other primary commodity prices, such as coconut-related products, lumber, and copper, have also affected other countries. Where the Philippines has specifically suffered from Marcos misrule economically has been the phenomenon known as "crony capitalism." In practice, while Marcos was in power, this involved the creation of paragovernmental marketing boards that established de facto commodity monopolies and undercut what would have been the beneficial impact of free market forces on recession-hit areas of the economy. At a time when sugar clearly had little future in the Philippines, Marcos cronies were authorized to set up fifteen new, government-financed sugar mills. Other commodities, like coconuts and bananas, were also put in the hands of Marcos appointees who, many suspected, then skimmed off sizable percentages for themselves and their friends.

Far more blatant examples of Marcos misappropriation of public funds may well emerge in the near future, particularly as full details emerge of the transfer overseas by Marcos and his wife of enormous sums of money derived from profiteering through their cronies. In the declining months of the Marcos era, the regime was as ill regarded by international finance as it was by Filipino business executives themselves. The International Monetary Fund imposed tight restrictions on the use of emergency credits made available to the Philippine government during 1985. In spite of this, Marcos borrowed heavily to finance the election campaign of his own political party, the KBL (initials for "New Society Movement" in Filipino). The borrowings, which amounted to $160 million by some estimates, violated IMF liquidity limits. Thus no better harbinger of an improved economic climate could be found in the first days of the Aquino regime than the healthy resurgence of the Manila stock market and the appreciation of the Philippine peso against foreign currencies.

To run the economy in the post-Marcos era, Aquino has appointed as finance minister a respected businessman with personal experience in commodity production, Jaime Ongpin, Harvard-educated president of the Benguet Mining Corporation. She has wisely kept in place the Marcos-appointed president of the Philippine Central Bank, the internationally respected Jose Fernandez. She has also called on the counsel, during the transition months of the early regime, of former Marcos Finance Minister and Prime Minister Cesar Virata. One of the very few Marcos ministers considered both free of the taint of corruption and personally able, Virata provided even the economic incompetence of Marcos rule with a veneer of respectability and seriousness.

To her credit, Mrs. Aquino acknowledges the severe limitations of her economic knowledge and experience, and is reported to have spent as much free time as she has had in the past few months boning up on economics. She clearly favors a classic, free-market approach to economic development, and has set as one of the new government's priorities the dismantling of the economically counterproductive and corruption-prone monopolies. Overall economic plans are still vague, but the new government understands the need to reverse investment priorities away from glamorous, high-capital urban projects to programs that will in the shortest possible time raise living standards at the very bottom of society in the countryside.

For Americans interested in doing business in the Philippines, President Aquino's new economic team is a promising group. Finance Minister Ongpin has set it as one of the priorities of the Aquino government to accelerate the flow of funds into the country. Ongpin strongly favors private sector investment over government projects, perhaps partly because of a reaction against the corruption that sprang up in the wake of Marcos-initiated grand development programs. Aquino's finance minister believes that a large amount of Filipino money that left the country during the dark economic days following the murder of Ninoy Aquino in 1983 will return. Minister of Trade and Industry Jose Concepcion has said: "The more control [by the government of business], the more chance of graft and corruption." Central Bank Governor Jose Fernandez, who was kept on by President Aquino because of the good job he had done in this position under Marcos, believes that the Philippine government may recoup some of its previously mishandled capital by selling off nonperforming assets in the form of factories that have been idle because of bankruptcy. Some of those factories were originally set up with loans made available to Marcos cronies by Marcos himself. President Aquino has pledged also to break up the government monopolies in coconut and sugar.

Still, she and her financial team are clearly wary of raising unrealistic expectations both at home and abroad of an instant turnaround in the country's economy. For all her appreciation of divine intervention, Corazon Aquino obviously still believes in old-fashioned methods of economic development. She cautions against impatience. "Here I am only two days and you people are expecting miracles," she told *Time*'s Hong Kong Bureau Chief Sandra Burton she had exclaimed to some followers who were complaining about the slow pace of change.

Two decades ago, the Philippines was one of the great growth hopes among developing countries in Asia, the original home of the so-called Green Revolution. Today, there is no illusion in the Aquino government that improved rice strains alone will quickly overcome rural indigence. But at least it is recognized that, if something is not done to raise the very lowest rural living standards, no amount of good government and honest democracy in the cities will save the Philippines from a tidal wave of revolutionary discontent. President Aquino has so far said little about how she proposes to raise the rural living standards in the Philippines. But she appears to believe strongly in both articulating and exemplifying moral principles as a way of motivating the hitherto disgruntled and oppressed of her country. On taking the presidential oath in February, the same day that Marcos was taking his "oath" as president, Aquino declared: "I am taking power in the name of the Filipino people. I pledge a government dedicated to upholding truth and justice, morality and decency, freedom and democracy."

The Marxist revolution in the countryside, in the early days of the Aquino regime, is still containable. Just as vigorous leadership, sound policies, and effective grass-roots implementation were able to contain and then turn back the Hukbalahap revolt of the early 1950s, so the same attributes could turn around the Philippine Communist rebellion of the 1980s. Today, as then, the rebellion has its roots in an interconnected web of causes, some of which are economic, some of which are political, and some of which are sociological. At bottom, the revolt would never have caught on as it has without a deterioration of the Philippine economic situation to near desperation point in some parts of the countryside, particularly in the islands of Samar, Mindanao, and Cebu, where the commodity recession has hit especially hard. Sugar, lumber, and coconut oil prices all slumped on the world market, putting hundreds of thousands of workers out of jobs.

In addition, despite some halfhearted attempts at land reform in the late 1940s and early 1950s, and then later in the early Marcos years, a large majority of the Philippine rural poor still eke out an existence as tenant farmers on insufficient land to support their families. Worse, in many places the long years of Marcos rule have made possible the reemergence of local strongmen-politicians, beholden only to Malacañang Palace, who have imposed an almost feudal-style rule on large regions of the countryside. This kind of provincial misrule has been further aggravated by the practice in some areas of political use of the local armed forces to silence criticism or opposition.

Communist recruiting has been a simple matter in these conditions. A frequent pattern has been a sort of ideological "softening-up" process in a target area by teams of students, radical priests and nuns, and human rights workers who, while not necessarily Communists themselves, have sympathized with the plight of the rural poor and Communist efforts to mobilize grass-roots political power out of it. The actual propagandizing, recruiting, and organizing has been done by cadres of the New People's Army, the armed wing of the Communist party of the Philippines. Altogether, estimates of full-time fighting strength of the NPA throughout the Philippines run from 15,000 to 20,000 armed guerrillas. These are believed to be scattered throughout as many as sixty-two of the nation's seventy-four provinces. Some U.S. military estimates have put NPA penetration of Filipino rural barrios (villages) at 20 percent or more.

Not surprisingly, the leadership of the Communist party of the Philippines (CPP) is composed almost entirely of alienated urban intellectuals, former students, professors, even a handful of professionals. Some probably would never have turned to armed rebellion at all if they had felt that there were alternative ways of improving conditions of Filipino society during the Marcos years. The party itself was formed only as recently as December 26, 1968 (Mao Zedong's birthday), by Jose Maria Sison, then a thirty-year-old lecturer at the University of the Philippines, and ten young followers discontented with what they considered an ineffective approach to revolution on the part of the old PKP (initials in Pilipino of Philippine Communist Party), the original Philippine Communist party of Soviet orientation. Sison and his followers were ardent Maoists, wholesale admirers of the Chinese Cultural Revolution, and believers in the efficacy of agrarian insurrection as the foundation of national Communist power. In March 1969, Sison and his newly formed party joined forces with a former Hukbalahap leader, Bernabe Buscayno, and together, the two and their followers founded the New People's Army. At its inception, this portentously named group numbered about threescore rebels and thirty-five or so assorted rifles and handguns.

Sison and Buscayno proved an effective combination of theoretician and guerrilla leader respectively, and followed a hallowed Communist tradition of choosing new names for themselves symbolic of their political intentions. Sison became Amado Guerrero and penned various tracts advocating "protracted people's war." Buscayno became known as Commander Dante. Both were active in guerrilla operations and organization until Buscayno's capture in 1976 and Sison's the following year, in Luzon. Until their release by the Aquino government in early March 1986, both had been held by the Marcos regime in prisons in Manila. Sison signed a document promising "not to seek to overthrow the government by violent means or force," but when repeatedly pressed to do so by journalists on the day of his release, refused specifically to renounce violence as a revolutionary tactic. A slim, smiling, almost shy individual, Sison found his leadership role in the party had clearly been eclipsed during his prison years, and the chairman of the party at the time of his release was Rodolfo Salas, a former engineering student.

To what extent the New People's Army is still authentically Maoist is not clear. Journalists who have visited the guerrillas in the field report that a rigid, ascetic discipline is imposed on the fighters. Men and women may not marry, for example, without express permission of party superiors. When they do marry, they are likely to be kept separate except for express conjugal times together also requiring party authorization. A cellular, self-replacing leadership structure evidently operates at Central Committee level, so that the party cannot be mortally wounded if key groups of leaders are arrested or killed.

As Sison has defined the objectives of the CPP and the New People's Army, they remain the overthrow of democratic government, which is allegedly characterized by "U.S. imperialism, feudalism, and bureaucrat capitalism." Captured CPP documents and reports by journalists who have studied the party and the New People's Army firsthand say that the ideology and methodology are an eclectic mix of classic Maoist rural-based revolutionary doctrine, sophisticated Soviet-style dialectics and party organization, and rural nativist fanaticism. Hatred of the United States appears to be inculcated at a very early stage of indoctrination of the peasantry, based on the premise that the United States is responsible for almost everything that is wrong with the Philippines and the world in general. Show trials and public executions play an important role in terrorizing doubters or potential government informers. Despite the alliance with the party of significant numbers

of left-leaning priests and nuns, the commitment to violence and
political terror seems unusually intense even by the murky standards of other past and present revolutionary movements in Asia.
Far from being "agrarian reformers" or well-meaning but misguided idealists, the hard core of the Communist party of the
Philippines may well be one of the most brutal, deceitful, and
dictatorial of any Marxist revolutionary group currently struggling
for power anywhere in the world outside of Kampuchea (the Khmer
Rouge) or Peru (the "Shining Path" revolutionaries).

President Aquino, who has admitted that economics and Communism are two of the subjects she knows least about, has clearly
taken a calculated risk, against the advice of her defense minister,
Juan Ponce Enrile, in ordering the release of both Sison and Buscayno, as well as two other top Communists, not to mention in
offering a six-month cease-fire with the Communist guerrillas as
a whole. She and Vice-President Salvador Laurel have expressed
the belief that, with Marcos out of office, a majority of those "in
the hills" — i.e., the Communists — can be inveigled back into
normal life. Laurel, for example, told U.S. business executives in
Manila in November 1985: "Given a credible government, democratic moral order and a general amnesty, ninety percent of the
people who are now fighting in the hills would lay down their
arms and come home." Cardinal Jaime Sin, the Philippine Roman
Catholic leader, says the same thing: "Some of them," meaning
the Communists, "are not Communists," and would, he feels,
"come down from the hills."

Whether this is an unduly optimistic analysis or not remains to
be seen. President Aquino's personal approach to the problems of
insurgency seems at least in part to be influenced by the revulsion
she feels for political incarceration as a whole in view of her hus-
band's imprisonment under Marcos. Her release of all Filipino
political prisoners held under Marcos, including Communist leaders considered dangerous by the Philippine military, clearly reflected this outlook. She also goes out of her way to refer to Christian
spiritual principles in describing the nature of her presidency and
what she is trying to do. Mrs. Aquino has been described by some

observers as almost "mystical" in her approach to government. In March 1986 she told Britain's *Economist* magazine that she believed that she became president because of a "miracle," a term she uses in its original meaning of intervention by God, not as a mere metaphor for an unlikely development. But Mrs. Aquino ought not to be underestimated because of that. In an interview with *Time*'s Sandra Burton, Aquino offered a revealingly clear-eyed assessment of what it takes to lead a nation. "I told Cardinal Sin," she explained, "that I can no longer be humble because people don't take me seriously then, so I have to project my confidence, even more than most men would. My philosophy is to do everything within your capability and then leave the rest to God. I have been honestly living that way since Ninoy's incarceration. No one can say Cory did not give it her all."

The predictions of Vice-President Laurel and Cardinal Sin about a weakening of the Communist insurgency in the event of an amnesty probably contain some truth. The problem of the insurgency is nevertheless more complicated merely than democracy on the one hand and people "in the hills" on the other. For one thing, it is now apparent that the CPP has successfully penetrated large areas of life in Manila itself. Much of the serious demonstrating in Manila and other major cities during the past few years against Marcos has been done by tough, highly indoctrinated student groups prepared to fight hard with the police and using such slogans as "Down with the U.S.–Marcos Dictatorship." The illegal — at least under Marcos — popular-front political arm of the Communists, the National Democratic Front (NDF), is a highly organized political mass action group with extensive contacts throughout Philippine urban life. Other leftist groups, such as Bayan, though not specifically Communist, have shown themselves willing to be allied with NDF political objectives, at least in the short term. Thus, regardless of how successful President Aquino is in improving rural conditions, reforming the military, and enticing rural guerrillas out of the countryside, some of the biggest political challenges her new regime may face could be from efforts by Communists both to infiltrate her own government and to create political splits within the broad popular coalition that swept her into power.

Assuming this is their goal, the Communists are likely to try hard to drive a wedge between Aquino and hard-liners — or sincerely anti-Communist reformists, for that matter — in the Philippine military establishment. One of the biggest dangers the New People's Army itself faces, assuming that it does not agree to a cease-fire, is from a post-Marcos, reformed, and revitalized military under competent field leadership. Aquino's newly appointed Chief of Staff Lieutenant General Fidel Ramos, a West Pointer, showed his own commitment to reform by firing twenty-two overage generals in his first week in office. If he is able to convince the more than 1,000 dedicated reformers in the Philippine officer corps of some 15,000 men that ability and professionalism will now be consistently rewarded above political factionalism, then the 230,000 armed services personnel the Philippine government can call upon could at last become effective in the fight against Communist insurgency.

Considerable military housecleaning will nevertheless be needed. Many Filipino military units are poorly trained and poorly disciplined, and contribute far more to social unrest than to social justice in the countryside. One of Ramos's highest military priorities should be to tighten the entire shape of the Philippine military, impose severe discipline on all acts of abuse of civilians, and reinstill pride and soldierly motivation. He will also have to find ways, as rapidly as possible, to repair the catastrophic decline of the Philippine armed forces' logistical capabilities. During the latter Marcos years, corruption and misappropriation of funds were so rife that today, according to a U.S. estimate, no more than 300 of the army's 700 trucks actually work. Presumably, the maintenance situation among army combat helicopters, vital for counterinsurgency work, is also little better. With a much cleaner Philippine administration, commitment by the Filipino defense establishment, and firm support and assistance by the United States, the problems can certainly be overcome.

Learning to cope with the new Aquino administration may prove frustrating at first for more gung-ho military officers in the Filipino military. If, for example, President Aquino declares a cease-fire against the NPA that is totally unreciprocated by the Communists, pressure from below on Ramos and Aquino to repudiate the cease-fire could be considerable. Many Filipinos, moreover, however grateful for the decisive role played by Defense Minister Enrile in ousting Marcos, have not forgotten Enrile's long years as keeper of martial law under Marcos and as successor-in-waiting there-after. Even the slightest friction between Enrile and Aquino could fuel renewed political uncertainty in the Philippines, perhaps urban unrest as well, and demands by some professional military men for a renewal of military rule.

A key role in trying to prevent this from happening is likely to be played by the Roman Catholic Church in the Philippines under its skillful and dynamic leader Cardinal Jaime Sin. The cardinal maintained a careful but basically adversarial political relationship with Marcos during the last half-dozen years or so of the Marcos regime, now chiding and criticizing it, now rebuking the more extreme critics of the government within the Church itself. Sin nonetheless was decisive in mobilizing "people power" to dem-onstrate in the streets against Marcos after the massive fraud per-petrated in the February 7, 1986, election. "Antitank nuns," as some women religious were whimsically called, were mobilized to stand between Marcos's armored columns and the Defense Min-istry where Enrile was leading a mutiny against Marcos, and then to present the embarrassed young soldiers with flowers. The Church's Radio Veritas was also important. For a while, it was alone in broadcasting political developments that the government did not want widely known.

Under the Aquino administration, Sin's role is likely to be quite different from what it was under Marcos. A witty and entertaining man (he calls his official residence "the house of Sin"), he was influential in December 1985 first in selecting Corazon Aquino as the anti-Marcos candidate of the united opposition and then in encouraging her to run hard against Marcos. The cardinal might now play an even more significant role in steering the rank and file of the Church's 13,000 priests and religious away from the flirtation of some of them with "liberation theology" and leftist violence and firmly behind political democracy as it is now re-emerging in the Philippines.

Trying hard to keep up with each new development in the heady first days of restored Filipino democracy will be a major challenge for the United States. American diplomats, military officers, and Reagan administration foreign policy analysts acquitted themselves well during the tense and difficult days leading to Marcos's ouster. Under the able leadership of U.S. Ambassador to the Philippines Stephen Bosworth, the embassy in Manila was informed in detail about important political developments as they happened, and its advice to Washington appears in retrospect to have been sensible and timely. American policy, moreover, was well served, after some initial fumbling by the White House, by a high degree of consensus throughout the U.S. government, both executive and legislative branches, that nothing short of Marcos's departure would ensure continued stable government in the Philippines.

That vigorous sense of direction and consensus in the U.S. government will be needed in abundance to guarantee that the Aquino administration establishes firm roots and has all of the resources it requires in order to begin pulling the Philippines back from the abyss of economic and political collapse. Washington at least started off on the right foot, easing Marcos out of power, getting him out of the country quickly and cleanly, and then assuring President Aquino of full political and financial support. For U.S. policy and interests in the Philippines to be fully served, though, a sustained level of energy and attention will have to be directed at the Philippines for months and years to come.

For a while during the crisis of Marcos's last days, there seemed to be some confusion in Washington whether its priority in the Philippines was the maintenance of the two U.S. bases or the reconstruction of Philippine democracy. In fact, the two goals are inseparable. An authoritarian regime of the right in Manila would before long provoke the sort of nationwide political and social unrest likely to bring on either civil war or, worse, a Communist revolution. Under either of these two likely outcomes, it would be difficult if not impossible to continue a U.S. military presence in the Philippines. Similarly, and obviously enough, any Communist-led regime in the country would almost certainly order the swift expulsion of Americans from Clark and Subic Bay and perhaps even invite their replacement by Soviet military personnel. This would be a disastrous prospect for the security of the entire Pacific Rim. No American policy directive for preserving the Philippine bases would make sense without listing at the outset the need to strengthen Philippine political democracy.

The bases themselves are, in the words of many U.S. military strategists, simply "irreplaceable." They are the largest U.S. military installations in any foreign country, and there is nothing even approaching them for size, comprehensiveness of facilities, or location anywhere in Asia. Assistant Secretary of Defense Richard Armitage has described their position athwart the Pacific sea-lanes and their range of capabilities as simply "unsurpassable." Both bases can project U.S. military power to as far away as the Persian Gulf and can oversee the Pacific Ocean choke-points through which eighty percent of the West's raw materials pass.

Subic Bay and its component naval airfield of Cubi Point provide deepwater support and logistics for the 80 ships and 550 aircraft of the U.S. Seventh Fleet. Four floating docks can accommodate surface ships or submarines. Subic's supply depot is the largest in the U.S. Navy, holding 3.8 million cubic feet of ammunition. With its total U.S. and Filipino workforce, skilled and unskilled, of 36,000, Subic is capable of keeping 70 U.S. Navy ships each month in good repair. Best of all, the cost for this high-level military support activity is only $70 a man-day, compared with approximately $420 in the United States.

Clark Air Base, the larger of the two U.S. bases, is hardly less valuable. The base is headquarters for the Thirteenth Air Force and its key component, the Third Tactical Fighter Wing. Its primary responsibility is for air defense throughout the Western Pacific and as far west as parts of the Indian Ocean. In essence, Clark is the main U.S. air defense base for the Philippines itself and Southeast

Asia. The base operates two F-4 Phantom squadrons and a squadron of F-5E fighters. The huge size of the base (131,000 total acreage) and its 46,000-acre bombing range provide unparalleled facilities outside of the mainland United States for combat flight training. Clark in particular makes use of its F-5E aircraft as an "aggressor squadron," painted in Soviet camouflage and trained in Soviet air combat tactics, in order to provide realistic opposition to U.S. fighter pilots during training exercises.

Clark and Subic Bay together have always played a vital role in U.S. strategic contingency planning in the Pacific Rim. With the growing Soviet presence at Cam Ranh Bay, on the coast of Vietnam, 750 miles away, they have become even more crucial to American defense planning for the region. Not least, Clark itself provides the Philippines with a credible perimeter defense that it could not possibly sustain on its own.

Under the current version of the Military Bases Agreement between the United States and the Philippines, signed in January 1979, the United States will be able to continue to use Clark and Subic until 1991 under an arrangement by which it pays "rent" of $180 million a year. The overall contribution of the bases to the Philippine economy is much bigger. They directly provide jobs for 53,200 Filipinos and inject an estimated $320 million into the Philippine economy each year.

About a year before Marcos was ousted from power, prospects for a continuation of the bases agreement after 1991 looked gloomy. Violent anti-Marcos street demonstrations and vituperative anti–U.S. rhetoric even from the ranks of the "moderate" democratic opposition appeared to be moving the post-Marcos Philippines onto a confrontation course with the United States. The largely nonviolent nature of the "Yellow Revolution," however, and the near-silence of the left during the key February days, did much to change this mood. Instead of insisting that the U.S. bases must "go" after 1991, President Aquino merely reiterated a careful campaign commitment to observe the agreement until 1991 and, before its expiration, reopen negotiations for the next period. She also referred vaguely to the possibility of a plebiscite on what Philippine policy should be on the bases.

Once installed as president, Mrs. Aquino said that she was "keeping [her] options open" on the bases after 1991 and would not commit herself to seeking either their continuation or their removal. Her vice-president, Salvador Laurel, in a no doubt deliberately off-the-cuff remark, later opined that he thought the bases might well be allowed by the Filipino people to continue if overall relations with the United States, as anticipated, were good. Mrs. Aquino did not object to this observation.

On the U.S. side, the goodwill toward the Philippines has always been considerable. With the exhilarating triumph of democratic sentiment in February 1986 in the country, that goodwill became, through an overwhelming, and in many respects rare, consensus of Americans, genuine affection and enthusiasm. "Try not to forget what you saw last week," *Time*'s essayist Roger Rosenblatt enjoined his readers in commenting on "People Power" in the Phillippines the week after Marcos fell. "It was ourselves," he added, "in eruption far away."

Perhaps just as important, a new generation of Filipino young people, some barely infants when Marcos declared martial law in 1972, saw the old and noble ideals of democratic government reintroduced in the vacuum left by a departing autocracy and given overwhelming encouragement, moreover, by the world's most experienced, and influential, free republic. It may be providential that even today, Filipinos are historically aware that twice in less than a century they have been liberated by Americans from foreign domination. Some 17,000 American young men lie buried in neat rows at the American cemetery at Fort Bonifacio outside Manila. Investment in blood for a common cause is a powerful cement among peoples. Even with the continuing bonds of culture and mutual familiarity, that cement will be needed by both countries to help ensure their mutual amity and, in a vital sense, each other's ultimate integrity as independent nations. Other Pacific Rim states should take note of this.

American business could play an important role in restoring confidence both between the United States and the Philippines and within the Philippines itself in the value of democratic rule and free market economics. Many overseas Chinese businessmen have already moved large amounts of capital back into the country on the grounds that the economy, after two years of absolute decline, has nowhere to go but up. There is, naturally, something of a chicken-and-egg conundrum about the Philippine economy. The country will attract foreign capital as it shows itself to be increasingly stable politically, and it will become increasingly stable as new capital can restore a sense of economic forward movement.

Careful economic and political judgment will be needed by President Aquino in what could become a surge of union-led labor disputes throughout the country. With full legality restored to labor union activity throughout the Philippines, there is obviously a risk of uncontainable demands for higher wages. There is also a chance that parts of the labor movement could be exploited for purely political purposes by the Philippines' Communists. American businesses will clearly have to weigh carefully the different factors before making long-range investment decisions. Yet if many executives of the talented Filipino business community are correct, a new period of economic growth, led by private capital investment, could be what follows the newly installed government of President Aquino. For all of the economic catastrophes of the past decade, the Philippines might yet reclaim its position as one of the economically hopeful countries on the Pacific Rim.

7

VIETNAM
Southeast Asia's Odd Man Out

IN *The Mouse That Roared*, a very funny movie starring the late British comic actor Peter Sellers, a tiny, Ruritanian-style European state declares war on the United States with the deliberate objective of losing. Its reasoning: countries that are defeated by the United States end up receiving massive amounts of economic aid.

In many ways, Vietnam today is the bitter reverse side of that sly truth. For the past ten years, since North Vietnamese divisions overran the entire southern half of Vietnam and imposed their rigid brand of Stalinist socialism upon the unified country, Hanoi has tasted the acrid fruit of "victory" over the United States. America was not militarily defeated, of course, as many Vietnamese Communists have freely admitted. But the political will of her people was broken in the course of a long and difficult conflict that was characterized on the U.S. side by the absence of a clear and attainable objective.

The wounds opened up by the war in the American psyche were very deep. Today many, perhaps most, Americans have simply not forgiven the Vietnamese for their role in causing them. For however misled or mistaken U.S. political leadership may have been in its Indochina policy between 1964 and 1975, the Hanoi regime relentlessly and mercilessly played upon every area of weakness and vulnerability in the American spirit. And it did so gloatingly and malevolently. In the United States the continuing sense of national hurt is reflected in the perennial debate over whether the war was "right" or not. But it is also displayed in the unusually stern determination by both U.S. government and private agencies to obtain from Hanoi a proper and final accounting of MIAs (and possibly POWs). That determination, moreover, has been part of a largely effective U.S. policy over the past decade of cutting Vietnam off from major commercial ties with the non-Communist world and helping to isolate the regime in the diplomatic sphere. It is, perhaps, one of the last of the Vietnam War's many ironies that the United States has been as diplomatically singled-minded and effective after the war's end as it was double-minded and pusillanimous when the conflict still raged.

The sense of Vietnam's isolation from the general concourse of nations is visibly plain on any visit to the country. To fly from, say, Manila to Hanoi is to enter both a different age and a different consciousness of life. For all of its economic and political troubles, the Philippines is recognizably a part of the international economy and the modern world, both good and bad parts of it. Yet in Vietnam the clock seems to have stopped a decade or more ago.

Some thirteen years after the last B-52 bombs rained down on Hanoi and Haiphong, the approach to Hanoi airport is still pocked with unfilled craters, the muddy punctuation marks of war amid the rice paddies. The airport itself is in a time warp. Lines of MiG-21 fighters salute the runway and the only large planes visible are likely to be a droop-winged Soviet Antonov transport, an Aeroflot or Czechoslovak Ilyushin-62, or a couple of Tupolev-134's that Hanoi employs to fly back and forth to Ho Chi Minh City. When the *Time* Newstour's chartered TWA Boeing 747SP landed at Hanoi airport, it was the first U.S. civilian airliner ever to touch down there. But it was also apparently the first wide-bodied airliner ever to land as well. The airport lacked a staircase big enough to reach the passenger doors, so a special set of stairs had to be welded in advance on top of the tallest conventional one available.

More than this almost touching backwardness, more than the

ancient Volga limousines waiting for VIPs on the airport apron, or the Soviet PAZ tourist buses, it is the countryside and the long road into Hanoi itself that set the tone for the visitor to Vietnam. A once beautiful, but now locked and crumbling Roman Catholic church is a reminder of crisper, more prosperous French colonial days. Barefooted peasants in the fields or on the roads, water buffaloes, and silent bicyclists bespeak not just a premodernization China of the 1960s but an India of two decades ago. Apart from the portentous motorcade of the foreign visitors, the only vehicles likely to be seen at all are military jeeps, a sprinkling of official Volgas, Soviet-made trucks, and, as the Newstour observed, a small convoy of SAM-2 antiaircraft missile transporters. The feeling of impoverishment is ubiquitous, and it is only confirmed when the bicycle traffic thickens on the outskirts of the city. There, and in the peeling, yellow stucco heart of Hanoi itself, a formerly elegant French colonial town, now dominated by bicycles, pedicabs, and pedestrians, a sense of decay gathers quietly around the visitor. "We think we are the poorest country in the world," declared Vietnamese Foreign Minister Nguyen Co Thach to visiting U.S. businessmen. Vietnam is not, but the country seems to wear its deprivation like a badge of political and moral rectitude.

The most obvious reason for Hanoi's poverty is war, and it is the reason Vietnamese leaders constantly cite in their hand-wringing laments over the state of their country. Vietnam, by both force of circumstance and deliberate choice, has been uninterruptedly at war with itself and its neighbors for forty years. With armed forces of 1.2 million, the fourth largest in the world, it is a mini-superpower in the world of conventional fighting. War seems to have entered the soul of at least the northern half of Vietnam like a political narcotic, simultaneously the means to political self-assertion within Indochina and the cause of its isolation outside it.

Some of the fighting was forced upon the Vietnamese. The French, for example, would have clung far longer than they did to a co-lonial Indochina if Ho Chi Minh and the Communist-led Viet Minh had not resorted to arms to force them out. Nationalist sentiment, under any political flag, was ready in Vietnam in 1945 to bring an end to the foreign presence — first the French, then the Japanese, and then the French again. But the seventeen-year war waged by Hanoi against the government of South Vietnam, however imperfect the Saigon regime was, was not a "national liberation" conflict in any meaningful sense of the word. It was part of the tapestry of political messianism woven into the minds of Ho Chi Minh and other Vietnamese Communist leaders from 1930 on, the year in which they founded, not the Vietnamese Communist party, but the Communist party of Indochina. It was the messianism, of course, that led them to resist the United States with extraordinary bravery and at terrible cost. It remains today the messianism that keeps four Vietnamese divisions garrisoned in neighboring Laos and some 170,000 troops engaged in pacification of the recalcitrant Khmer Rouge. The Vietnamese Communists believe in their bones that it is their destiny to direct events in the Indochina Peninsula. They do not like to say this to outsiders, but Vietnamese Communist internal literature, both published and secret, has consistently proclaimed as much for half a century.

What today's leaders of Vietnam do attempt is half denial and half defense of their Indochina behavior. At a luncheon in Hanoi for visiting American business executives in November 1985, Foreign Minister Thach explained that the Vietnamese had founded the Communist party of Indochina in 1930 because the Vietnamese "had to have the organization to fight against the French. The Indochinese Communist party," he added, "was not from our initiative, but from the French." (In fact, it was neither French nor Vietnamese initiative, but Soviet, for Ho Chi Minh was at the time the principal Communist agent in Indochina of the Comintern, Stalin's organizational device for asserting control over the world Communist movement.) Thach claimed that there had not been "a single word" on a possible Federation of Indochina (the original Communist Vietnamese political proposal for post-French Indochina) since 1950. More revealingly, he went on to compare the current Vietnamese occupation of Cambodia with the occupation by the Allies of conquered Germany after World War II. "If (the Soviet Union, Great Britain, and the United States) have the right to go up to Berlin to crush Hitler," he asked rhetorically, "why do we have no such right to go up to Phnom Penh to crush Pol Pot?" As for the Vietnamese divisions in Laos, Thach added: "We'll leave Laos any time the Laotians ask the Vietnamese to leave, as they asked the Vietnamese to leave in 1975."

Despite Thach's disclaimers, the record of Vietnamese Communist behavior toward its then non-Communist neighbors during the late 1960s and early 1970s confirms over and over again the attitude of political superiority that has characterized the world view of the Hanoi regime ever since the ascendancy of Ho Chi Minh in the 1940s. The fall of Cambodia to the Khmer Rouge, for example, would never have taken place without Vietnamese assistance in the critical early months of 1970 to the still poorly armed Khmer Communist forces. But the overthrow of Sihanouk, which led to the widening of the war in Cambodia, was not, as has often been claimed or implied, chiefly the result of misguided U.S. military tactics. It grew directly out of flagrant abuse of Cambodian "neutral" territory by North Vietnamese regiments infiltrating south across Cambodia into South Vietnam. Sihanouk was in Moscow when he was overthrown by General Lon Nol in March 1970. His mission there, as he told the French press in Paris, was to protest to the Soviets the North Vietnamese use of Cambodia as "a game reserve." Similarly, it was the Vietnamese who bore the brunt of the fighting in Laos against Laotian government forces — also designated "neutralist" — in the Vietnamese-inspired and ultimately successful efforts of the Laotian Communists, the Pathet Lao, to overthrow the legal regime of Prince Souvanna Phouma in August 1975.

Today, Vietnamese domestic literature continues to make it clear that Hanoi regards the survival of its own "revolution" as integral with everything that takes place in Kampuchea (formerly known as Cambodia) and Laos. In a December 1984 issue of the theoretical organ of Hanoi's armed forces, Le Duc Anh, commander of Vietnamese forces in Kampuchea, openly describes Indochina as "one theater of operations" for his own forces. He adds: "If at any time the block of solidarity and alliance among the three countries were not firmly maintained, the revolution in the three countries would not be able to avoid difficulties and losses." At the same time, the Vietnamese are profoundly conscious that others read their own literature and that their political motives are suspect throughout the region. They are thus defensive about their actions. Thach, ever the smooth diplomat, sought to allay these fears with his Newstour visitors. "Some people say we are used to war. This is not true," he protested. "Some people say we are the Prussians of the East. But, you see, we are a victim of war."

If that is so, then Vietnam must surely be considered a victim of its own ideology as well. More than anything else, certainly more than nationalism alone, it is the ideology, a particularly strident brand of Marxism-Leninism, that both has shaped the grim conditions of life in post-1975 Vietnam and continues to supply Hanoi with a rationale for all of its actions outside its own borders. What in the past made this particularly hard for many Americans to understand — at least before the exodus of the boat people in the late 1970s — were the seductively appealing slogans of the North Vietnamese propaganda fronts employed by Hanoi to undermine American political resistance to eventual takeover of the South by North Vietnam. For most of the 1960s, Hanoi propaganda about its objectives for South Vietnam was proclaimed through the National Liberation Front, a supposedly independent South Vietnamese organization dedicated to the rule of justice and law after the overthrow of the South Vietnamese government. The 1960s platform of the NLF, indeed, reads like the very model of Wilsonian civic virtues. Included are promises of "freedom of expression, assembly and association, travel, religion and other democratic liberties . . . a general amnesty for all political detainees," and, of course, the prohibition of "illegal arrests, illegal imprisonment, torture, and corporal punishment."

The NLF was supposed to have assumed power in South Vietnam after the "revolution" had taken place. In fact, the decision to abandon all pretense of Southern independence from the North was made at a long political meeting of the Hanoi Politburo at the South Vietnamese hill station of Dalat in the summer of 1975.

Ideologist Truong Chinh set the tone for the new move. "Marxism-Leninism," he proclaimed, "the apex of human thought, is playing a leading role in society, and the socialist culture, imbued with a national and popular character, is expanding. New-type socialist men imbued with patriotism and proletarian internationalism, and with socialist virtues, are in the making." Hanoi's real objective in waging war against South Vietnam — namely, to create a Stalinist unitary state — had, of course, never wavered, even during the protracted "peace" negotiations with the United States from 1968 onward. When, in 1974, there was some concern in Hanoi that the Peace Agreement concluded the previous year with the United States had brought setbacks to the North Vietnamese political timetable, a Politburo meeting was secretly convened in Hanoi from September 30 to October 8. Le Duan, then the First Secretary of the Vietnamese Communist party ("Indochinese" became "Vietnamese" in 1945), laid down the clinching argument for the peace accords. They provided, he said, "a strategic opportunity for completely liberating the South."

The general outline of such "liberation" became well known in the outside world over the next half-decade. Approximately 700,000 Vietnamese fled from the South in rickety boats across the South China Sea to precarious refugee way stations in Malaysia, Thailand, Hong King, and the Philippines. Others made it overland to China or Thailand. Thousands of the women who avoided drowning on the sea trip were nonetheless raped by pirates, many repeatedly. The men were robbed again and again, or thrown overboard if they attempted to prevent the violation of their womenfolk. An estimated 110,000 refugees either drowned at sea or were murdered by Thai pirates. But still they came, fleeing a society that was being purged politically and collectivized economically to the point of insanity. By 1980 some 80 percent of Vietnam's estimated 182,000 ethnic Chinese population had been driven out by the economic conditions, thousands of them fleeing across the northern border of Vietnam to southern China. Altogether, more than one million Vietnamese had fled their homeland after its "liberation" by fellow Vietnamese.

During the first years of Hanoi rule over the South, hundreds of thousands of former South Vietnamese officers and soldiers were incarcerated in "reeducation" camps intended to change their political convictions through the usual devices of semistarvation and psychological bullying. According to one academic investigation undertaken at the University of California at Berkeley, political executions may have amounted to some 65,000. Today, many of the former South Vietnamese prisoners have been released from reeducation, though eleven years after the war's end an estimated 60,000, according to State Department estimates, are still held. Hanoi claims that this figure is only 7,000. Some Vietnamese still attempt to flee their homeland by sea, despite the appalling risks, but an "orderly departure program" provides others with a legal way of departing and reaching the United States or Western Europe, provided they have close relatives willing to sponsor them and are prepared to wait, if necessary, several years. Vietnam's premier, Pham Van Dong, has expressed regret about this situation. "This is a sorrowful matter for us," he said to visiting Americans, "to have Vietnamese leave their country for abroad." Astonishingly, he declared, "most of them will come back to their fatherland."

That is highly unlikely, given Vietnam's present condition. The war, of course, did indeed devastate much of Vietnam, both North and South. Yet except for some rocketing and artillery shelling at the very end, in April 1975, Saigon itself was largely untouched by the fighting. Hanoi was heavily bombed, but with impressive precision, to judge by a drive through the city center, which shows hardly any evidence at all even of the massive "Christmas bombing" by U.S. B-52s in 1972. The Vietnamese civilian population, of course, suffered enormously during the Vietnam War. The fact is, nevertheless, that the physical devastation of the urban areas of both North and South Vietnam never compared with the utter devastation visited upon Seoul, for example, during the Korean War. The impoverishment of Vietnam today, though it has been aggravated by flooding and other natural disasters, is very largely a man-made phenomenon, the result of the imposition of economic policies that generate capital formation only at exceptionally high human cost, and that are demonstrably incapable of creating ordinary prosperity.

The cruel doctrinaire approach to economics was applied to South Vietnam almost before the North had any notion of the kind of society it was taking over. In 1975 alone, some 400,000 inhabitants of Saigon — excluding the thousands being dispatched for "reeducation" — were sent out to the countryside to poorly conceived and often unworkable "New Economic Zones." In some cases, urbanites were virtually dumped off trucks in jungle clearings and told to prepare their own accommodations out of nothing. As Hanoi officials later admitted, some 60 percent of the coerced urban emigrants had surreptitiously returned within a few months. There are no official figures of those who died of starvation, disease, or exposure during this reckless experiment.

The real crunch came in 1978 and 1979. In 1978, the Politburo in Hanoi decided to abolish all "capitalist remnants" in the South — in effect, to eliminate some 30,000 private retail stores. This decision may or may not have been motivated by a suspicion of disloyalty among Vietnam's ethnic Chinese, but the effect of the new ruling was to fall most heavily upon the members of the Chinese community, who had thrived — as they have always done in Southeast Asia — in urban retail activities. In 1978 and 1979, more than 150,000 ethnic Chinese left Vietnam, most of them going to China, but many going across the perilous ocean to Thailand or Malaysia. The year after the decision was promulgated, Hanoi instituted agricultural collectivization throughout South Vietnam. In 1979 alone, some 13,240 collectives had been established, with an average area of 40 to 50 hectares. As usual, coercion was employed to force the reluctant peasantry into the new organizations. By the end of 1980, nearly 10,000 of the collectives had collapsed.

Inevitably, Vietnam's food situation became dire during the first five years of such Stalinist social engineering. Grain production actually declined during 1976–1978, going from 13.6 million tons in 1976 to 12.2 in 1978. In this last year, in fact, Vietnamese had much less to eat than they had during the height of the war. Mass starvation was averted only by importing 1.5 million tons of grain from the eastern bloc. In August 1979, paradoxically at the height of the collectivization, the authorities allowed a de facto contract system to operate in the countryside, and the result was a significant improvement in agricultural yields. By 1983, according to Foreign Minister Thach, Vietnam was once again on the verge of rice self-sufficiency, but natural calamities in the following two years once more cut into production and overall living standards.

"Self-sufficiency" itself is a term that should be treated with some skepticism. Vietnam's population growth, according to the Hanoi authorities today, is approximately 2.25 percent, a rate of increase that is far outstripping agricultural output. In 1983, according to a candid assessment by the Vietnam Institute of Nutrition, average calorie intake in Vietnam as a whole was merely 1,940 per person per day. In addition, the institute noted that protein intake was too low. It recommended a minimum daily 2,100 calorie consumption for the 1986–1990 Five Year Plan. It gave no indication how such an increase was to be accomplished. Compared with the average recommended daily calorie intake in Western countries (approximately 2,500 to 3,750 for adult males, depending on the degree of activity of daily work), the figures were extremely low.

Hanoi's authorities have tacitly acknowledged that their economic policies for the first five postwar years were disastrously counterproductive, though they have never admitted the obvious, namely, that in Asia as in the rest of the world, doctrinaire Marxist insistence upon total collectivization of food production is a recipe for economic disaster. The disruptions, the collectivization, and of course the war with China in 1979 and with Kampuchea from 1978 until today have also bogged the Vietnamese economy down even more than it would already have been by the straitjacket of Stalinist socialism.

With the spread of the contract system in the early 1980s and an easing up of the pace of collectivization, Vietnam's economy did finally begin to grow at a respectable rate. This, according to

Vietnamese authorities, was 7.7 percent annually between 1981 and 1984, compared with the previous half-decade average annual figure of 0.2 percent. By the end of 1985, there was strong evidence that the Vietnamese hoped this might lead to American business pressures on the U.S. government to end its current trade embargo with the Hanoi regime.

Stressing carefully that the Newstour was purely on a fact-finding mission, the participants showed no direct interest in buying from or selling to Vietnam. Such an attitude of caution by U.S. business representatives, even aside from the U.S. government embargo on trade, is at the very least prudent. Vietnam's economic policies have still not stabilized, even though there is a clear reluctance to return to the dogmatic collectivization of the 1970s. The black market thrives, despite everything; or perhaps, because of everything, it has to thrive. Many Vietnamese — according to some estimates, as many as 200,000 — survive at all only because of packages sent from abroad containing items that they can sell for food. Duty on these essential gifts can vary from 15 percent to 200 percent. Yet the practice makes Hanoi uneasy, not just because it is an open rebuke to the efficacy of socialist economic doctrine, but because it creates yet another economic activity that the authorities have difficulty controlling.

In September 1985, the government suddenly devalued the currency, the dong, requiring that old 10-dong notes be replaced by new ones of one dong. Families were permitted to change only 2,000 dong each. According to Tran Quynh, vice-chairman of Hanoi's Council of Ministers, there was a need to cope with counterfeit money that had been brought into Vietnam in large quantities. But an equally cogent reason for the change was to prevent the buildup by any families of capital that might be used to finance other economic activities or even such illegal moves as fleeing from the country. To ensure that the measures were as effective as possible, all flights from Saigon were suspended during the exchange. The black market currency rate, meanwhile, soared to 1,000 old dong to the U.S. dollar. The official rate at the time was 100 dong to one U.S. dollar.

In Saigon, officials are clearly aware of the poor state of Vietnam as a whole and of the need for encouragement of free enterprise and commercial activity. Visiting Americans have been quietly told that Saigon desperately needs an injection of commercial capital and the opportunity to use it effectively. One Saigon official told a U.S. businessman: "We need more foreign enterprise. That's the only way to get this city working." The same man then confided that he would like to get to San Francisco and "see the interesting things of [the American] system." The whole mood of the South, of course, is different from the North; living standards, though slipping from their pre-1975 level, are still much higher than those in the North. Hanoi Communist cadres being transferred South on duty often describe the move as "going to heaven."

It is one thing for Saigon's Hanoi-appointed and, in senior instances, Hanoi-originated officials to confide entrepreneurial aspirations to visiting foreigners, especially when they are sure that no one else is listening. It is something different for the old men running the Politburo in Hanoi to acknowledge that any of the doctrines and theories they have tenaciously embraced for the past half-century need revising, not to mention discarding. In Hanoi in 1985, Premier Pham Van Dong was questioned closely and critically by American visitors about his country's obsession with economic collectivism as the best way to national prosperity. He was none too gently reminded that the economic performance of all of his Southeast Asian neighbor-states, even with allowances made for Vietnam's war losses, had consistently outstripped Vietnam's dismal deeds. Dong, often scowling arrogantly at his questioners or laughing at their ideas, was totally uncompromising about his country's economic posture. "We have the best model to build our country," he assured them. "We have chosen the best path to advance. I would like to bet you that by the year 2000, you will see it. We shall see each other [then]." The Vietnamese premier will have to overcome strong contrary actuarial forces to fulfill his promise: he is eighty years old.

Perhaps the only comparably rigid Communist party leadership anywhere in the world is in North Korea, yet another state with pronounced hegemonistic leanings. When Kim Il-sung leaves the scene, there is at least the possibility of a change, even if his still untested son, Kim Jong-il, takes over. But in Vietnam it will not be enough merely for Premier Pham Van Dong, once referred to by Ho Chi Minh as "my other self," to die. It will be necessary for an entire generation of comrades-in-arms of Ho Chi Minh, all in their seventies and eighties, to leave the scene before any reasonable change in Hanoi's policies can be anticipated. Men like First Secretary Le Duan, for example, seventy-nine, and Chairman of the State Council Truong Chinh, also seventy-nine, have shared in the key decisions of Vietnamese Communist life for the past forty years. Ho Chi Minh and they all drew their political ideology from the version of Marxism-Leninism that was imparted by Stalin to Communists around the world in the 1930s and 1940s.

There are, meanwhile, powerful geopolitical reasons for the unlikelihood of any major alteration of Vietnam's domestic and foreign policies in the immediate future. During the 1960s and 1970s, while fighting the South Vietnamese and the United States, Hanoi sought diligently to steer a course equidistant between China and the Soviet Union. Two factors made this course impossible to continue soon after the formal unification of North and South Vietnam in 1976. The first was the outbreak of hostilities between the increasingly pro-Chinese and anti-Vietnamese Khmer Rouge of Pol Pot in 1978. The hostilities were initiated by the Khmer Rouge in Kampuchea, but they led to the Vietnamese invasion of Kampuchea, which in turn led to China's own invasion of Vietnam in February 1979. The second factor was the sheer inability of the Hanoi regime to generate enough funds from the country's economy to keep its own people from starving, much less to sustain a counterinsurgency war. Both factors compelled the Vietnamese to lean heavily toward the Soviet Union.

Since then, Moscow has provided an estimated $2 billion a year in economic and military assistance to Hanoi, an amount equal to approximately 25 percent of Vietnam's GNP. Without this help, the Vietnamese economy would have been close to complete collapse and widespread starvation might have ensued. In return for this act of bailing out, which will continue into the foreseeable future, Hanoi has paid a steep price in terms of control over its own territory. The American-built deep-water port of Cam Ranh Bay in Central South Vietnam is now the most important Soviet military base outside the Warsaw Pact. Since May 1985, the Soviets have had complete administrative control over the base, whose port can handle thirty naval units daily, including nuclear fast-attack submarines, and whose airfield is used by Soviet MiG-23 fighter-bombers and Tu-95 Bear reconnaissance aircraft capable of far-reaching surveillance over the South China Sea and much of the western Pacific. Other Soviet aircraft fly in and out of Da Nang, another base built by the United States. An estimated 10,000 Soviets live and work in Vietnam as advisers to the Vietnamese government or as military personnel.

It is revealing to note that though the Soviets are permitted to move freely around North Vietnam, their movements are restricted in southern Vietnam, probably because of their unpopularity. There have been several reports, not confirmed by the Vietnamese or the Soviets, that, as part of the payback provisions for Soviet support, batches of Vietnamese workers have been sent, at token wages, to help build the huge new Trans-Siberian rail project, known in the Soviet Union as the BAM (for Baikal-Amur Railroad). Moscow, of course, may find the Vietnamese as intransigent and difficult to deal with in the role of allies as the United States and China have found them in the role of enemies. The Chinese have proclaimed that the Vietnamese occupation of Kampuchea is the most serious of the "three obstacles" in the way of improved Sino-Soviet relations. The occupation, which has gone on since the initial Vietnamese invasion of December 1978, is one of the world's longest-running antiguerrilla campaigns. It is doubtful whether Hanoi estimated, when it originally launched its massive assault on the Khmer Rouge regime in Kampuchea, that it would still be suppressing rural insurgents eight years later.

Thus if Soviet Communist party chief Mikhail Gorbachev decides to make Soviet-China rapprochement a foreign policy priority, he may well lean on Hanoi to make a political compromise over Kampuchea. The Vietnamese, though, will still have a card to play. Their 650,000 troops along the Sino-Vietnamese border may so provoke the Chinese as to bring down a new Chinese invasion of Vietnam — in effect the long-threatened and long-postponed Chinese "second lesson" to Vietnam. In this eventuality, unlikely though it appears at present, the Soviets will have no alternative but to give renewed public support to the Vietnamese.

Vietnam's leaders have protested vigorously that they seek better relations with China, an assertion that, from their own perspective, is certainly a genuine one. The enormous static defense they must maintain along their northern border is yet another drain on their already stretched financial resources. Premier Pham Van Dong put it earnestly. "From the bottom of our hearts," he proclaimed, "we'd like to resume talks with China to improve relations between the two countries, because normalization of relations between Vietnam and China is beneficial to both countries and to this nation as a whole. But I have to tell you that, as of this day, China has not shown any goodwill." Foreign Minister Nguyen Co Thach expressed similar feelings in a more detached vein. "China is too big," he said, "and Vietnam is very small. China is twenty times bigger than Vietnam. So every policy [adopted by Vietnam] bears on the Vietnamese character. And the policy of China must bear on its national history and character."

So far, China has responded only grumpily to such overtures. In September 1985 it flatly denied rumors emanating from Hanoi that the two sides had entered into secret talks to improve diplomatic relations. The Chinese foreign ministry spokesman tartly argued that since Vietnam was "continuing its aggression against and occupation of Kampuchea, there [was] no point in talking with it." Official statements out of Peking early in 1986 were even more ominous, not directly threatening a Chinese retaliation for alleged Vietnamese border provocations, but implying the approach of a point of no return once again in the uneasy relationship.

It is not just the problems with China and the ongoing war in

Kampuchea that make Vietnam such a volatile element in the Indochina peninsula and Southeast Asia as a whole. Despite flat, blank-faced denials by Hanoi (said Premier Pham Van Dong in November 1985: "We have never intruded and will never intrude into Thai territory"), Vietnamese troops have repeatedly crossed the border into Thailand in hot pursuit of Khmer Rouge and non-Communist Khmer rebel groups fighting them and the Vietnamese-installed Heng Samrin regime. Thai civilian and military lives have been lost, property has been damaged, and Thai territory has even temporarily been occupied on a number of occasions. As long ago as 1974, when Thai troops captured in Laos during the war against the Vietnamese-supported Pathet Lao returned from imprisonment in North Vietnam, they reported that their captors had told them that one day Vietnamese blood would be "flowing in the veins of Thailand." Even making allowances for the hyperbole of Vietnamese POW interrogators, the words are not inconsistent with the hubristic revolutionary self-image of the Vietnamese regime.

They also accord with a world view that sees enemies virtually everywhere. Quite seriously, Foreign Minister Thach assured an American audience in Hanoi that there was "no guarantee" that Japan would not have a huge army within ten to fifteen years. Thus, he asserted, "the great concern of every Asian country is the threat from China and the threat from Japan." Regrettably for the overall cohesiveness of ASEAN foreign policy, Hanoi has found some sympathy for its views in Indonesia, where suspicion of China is intense and rooted in the traumatic events of the Indonesian coup of 1965, which brought President Suharto to power. Indonesians have also shown more outright antipathy to Japan over the past two decades than any other Southeast Asian country, a sentiment at least partly due to Japan's disproportionate contribution (more than 40 percent) to Indonesia's import bill.

Given all this, it is clear that Hanoi would regard the establishment of normal diplomatic relations with the United States as a diplomatic achievement of major significance. Recognition by Washington and the elimination of the trade embargo would make it difficult, if not impossible, for the ASEAN countries to maintain their frosty estrangement from Hanoi. It might also add an additional inhibition to any Chinese thoughts of major new hostilities with Vietnam. Pham Van Dong informed American visitors that improved American-Vietnamese relations was yet another topic close to "the bottom of [his] heart." He then reminded them of the allegedly "lost golden chance" of 1945, when American OSS officers first made contact with Ho's Vietminh guerrillas fighting the Japanese and seemed sympathetic to their aspirations for independence from the French. He added: "We think that our relations with the U.S. in various ways are not only in our own interest but in the interests of the U.S. This is due to the geopolitical conditions. Am I right? Do you have any objections?" Then, bullyingly, when none of his audience commented, he concluded, "Silence means contempt?" At another point, "The door is open," he observed. "Why don't you come in?"

The United States in fact very nearly walked through "the door" of relations with Vietnam during the Carter administration in 1978. The Vietnamese even designated a spacious, lime-colored house and compound on Hanoi's Ha Ba Trung Street as the future U.S. embassy. Negotiations fell apart, however, during the simultaneous developments of U.S. negotiation for normalization of relations with Peking late in 1978 and the sudden worsening of Vietnamese-Kampuchean and Vietnamese-Chinese relations. During the first three years of the Reagan administration, there was a definite retreat by the U.S. side from an earlier position favoring a rapprochment with Hanoi. Washington was, for one, becoming alarmed by Vietnamese incursions into Thailand and by the cat-and-mouse game Hanoi appeared to be playing over the issue of accounting for American MIAs in Indochina. The nadir of relations was probably reached in September 1983, when Secretary of State Shultz said that Vietnam had "isolated itself by its actions" and that its international behavior was "outside the pale." Assistant Secretary of State Elliot Abrams also termed the Vietnamese government "the single most repressive regime in the world."

The official U.S. position is that relations between Washington and Hanoi will not be normalized until the United States is satisfied that Hanoi has done its very best to account for the 2,441 men officially listed as missing in action during the U.S. involvement in Indochina. The MIA issue is, for understandable reasons, extremely sensitive in the American domestic political climate and in no way one that could, or should, be simply brushed under the carpet of broader U.S. strategic interests in improving relations with Hanoi. For one thing, it is a major test of overall Vietnamese credibility. There is a strong suspicion in Washington, and throughout the United States, in fact, that Hanoi has cynically kept in reserve various remains of dead U.S. servicemen as a bargaining chip to secure its own interests in discussions with Washington. There is also a widespread belief, occasionally fed by reports that the State Department is usually unwilling to refute categorically, that live Americans — unreported POWs, in effect — have been spotted in Vietnam or Laos.

Officially, the Vietnamese deny that they hold any Americans involuntarily or that they have not been forthcoming about the MIA issue. "We consider the MIA issue a humanitarian question," claimed Thach in November 1985. The Vietnamese have nevertheless taken a major step forward in meeting U.S. demands for a proper accounting of the MIA question by agreeing to resolve the issue within two years.

There are other unmistakable indications of seriousness on Hanoi's part in breaking down U.S. objections to diplomatic and commercial normalization. In January 1986, the highest-ranking U.S. official delegation into Hanoi since the end of the Vietnam War made substantial progress in arranging new joint American-Vietnamese excavations of possible MIA sites. Led by Assistant Secretary of State Paul F. Wolfowitz and Assistant Secretary of Defense Richard L. Armitage, the Americans found the Vietnamese evidently eager to wrap up the whole MIA question as soon as possible. Despite warm cordiality surrounding these discussions, however, the United States said that it would still not open a representative office in Hanoi — an "interests section" formally attached to another foreign embassy, for example, to function as a diplomatic presence just short of diplomatic relations as such — until Vietnam had continued to show "a sustained pattern of cooperation." Ironically, on the very day that the U.S. delegation was arriving in Hanoi, a legal suit was brought in Fayetteville, North Carolina, against the CIA and the U.S. embassy in Bangkok by former U.S. servicemen convinced that there had been a coverup by Washington officials of information about MIAs and POWs. Assistant Secretary of Defense Armitage characterized the charge as "specious and absurd."

There are surely no compelling reasons for swift U.S. normalization of relations with Hanoi. The argument that the United States might, by making available large amounts of aid to Hanoi, be able to wean Vietnam away from Moscow is a flimsy one. It presumes such a change of heart by Hanoi about its ideological and strategic preferences as to go against the entire grain of half a century of Vietnamese Communist history. It also presumes a mood of benevolence toward Vietnam that does not characterize the present mood of the Senate and House of Representatives. The commercial benefits to the United States of open trade with Hanoi are also dubious at present. For one thing, Vietnam has hardly any hard currency to buy products the United States might be willing to sell, and it has little to offer to the U.S. market. Vice-Chairman of the Council of Ministers Tran Quynh told the U.S. businessmen in Hanoi in 1985 that Vietnam could export coal, tea, shrimp, rubber, coffee, lobsters, vegetables, and fine arts. In return, he said Vietnam was interested in importing oil, fertilizer, chemicals, insecticides, cotton, steel, machinery, and automobiles. Under an "open door" economic policy similar to that obtaining at present in China, Vietnam might presumably be a tempting market for some U.S. exporters. At present, the prospects look dim.

But there are more important reasons why the United States ought to let "a decent interval," perhaps a few more years, elapse before conferring upon Hanoi the respectability of a U.S. embassy. The Vietnamese have announced that they will withdraw from Kampuchea by 1990 regardless of developments there. They should be given a chance to live up to that commitment and the United

States ought to use it as a bargaining chip for diplomatic recognition. Meanwhile, even as they lie repeatedly about their military incursions into Thailand, the Vietnamese remain a dangerous destabilizing element affecting the future of the most important U.S. ally on the Southeast Asian mainland. Hanoi has even at times hinted that it will, through Laos, reignite the embers of Thailand's own Communist insurgency in the northeast of that country, a rebellion that the Chinese supported in the 1960s and early 1970s. When Peking cut off support to its Southeast Asian Maoist client rebellions, and when Bangkok itself adopted an effective amnesty policy toward the insurgency, the rebellion died on the vine. Hanoi, if it chose, could nevertheless create serious internal security headaches for the Thais. With such an inherent threat, U.S. diplomatic recognition of Hanoi might thus prove to be seriously unnerving for the Bangkok regime.

Finally, there are cogent U.S. domestic reasons for letting the healing hand of passing years rest upon American-Vietnamese relations before the civilities of diplomacy are entered into. Though, as Sir Winston Churchill once observed, the purpose of diplomatic recognition is "to secure a convenience, not to confer a compliment," the "convenience" of American-Vietnamese normalization may be outweighed by the still unresolved bitterness between the two nations. Vietnam's present, aging leadership remains rigid, vituperative, and self-righteous about its war with the United States. The angry, boastful display in Hanoi's Army Museum has, in the section dealing with the U.S. war in Vietnam, glass cases with the accoutrements of captured or dead American pilots: flight helmets with their squadron insignia, flying boots, pilot I.D. cards, the contents of survival packs. Photos of close-shaven, pajama-clad American POWs are prominently mounted on a large, cross-shaped backing in the center of the display. "Why the shape of the cross?" we asked the self-assured Vietnamese officer, a veteran of the war against the South. "Because it is a sign of defeat," he replied without further explanation.

Even though such arrogant sentiments probably do not reflect the thinking of ordinary Vietnamese toward the United States in general and Americans in particular, the fact that they have been officially blessed by Hanoi would serve as a serious psychological and political block in the way of any truly constructive U.S.–Vietnam diplomacy. More important, the still passionate feelings on the part of many Americans that the United States was right to try to help South Vietnam and neutral Laos against the cold-blooded war of conquest by the North and that the 58,022 Americans who died fell in a worthy cause should also be respected. Future historians will certainly assign praise or blame for the U.S. actions in Vietnam far more impartially than anyone can now. Today, though, those Americans who lost husbands, sons, or brothers in the conflict would justifiably feel outraged if Washington were to pretend diplomatically that it no longer mattered whether Hanoi's proven warlikeness had been tempered by time — and opposition — or not. Vietnam as a nation and a people certainly has its own legitimate interests in the Pacific Rim community. For the time being, though, most of that community disagrees profoundly with Vietnam over which of the country's professed interests are legitimate. In that sense, Vietnam remains Asia's odd man out. There is little likelihood in the foreseeable future of its movement away from that role or of American commercial involvement in the country.

8

THAILAND
Linchpin of the Southeast

THE NAME "Thailand" literally means "Free Land." Alone of all the countries in Asia, Thailand has never been dominated by a colonial European power. For Thailand itself, national independence is a powerful emotion. As Thais love to remind foreigners, for 800 years, the country, though briefly conquered by the Burmese, was substantially independent. During the period of French domination over Indochina and British domination over Burma and Malaya in the nineteenth century, Thailand skillfully maintained its political freedom from each of these major powers. The Thais conceded just enough in matters of trade and territorial disputes to head off potentially dangerous military confrontations with the Europeans, and their kings proved adept at modernizing sufficiently to prevent fatal political and social corrosion from within.

That openness to compromise and flexibility distinguishes Thailand from, say, the Confucian-influenced culture of the Vietnamese, Chinese, and Koreans, or the samurai competitiveness of the Japanese. Some sociologists have used the term "soft culture" to describe it. Less kind observers have noted that, while the Thais favored the regionally predominant but relatively benevolent British during the nineteenth century, their national flexibility also led them to support the entirely unbenevolent Japanese during World

War II. The Thais have simply maintained their independence by not clashing head-on with more powerful neighbors and by placating the regionally dominant powers. Today, they are given strong support in their rivalry with Vietnam by China, which has provided the bulk of the weaponry for the Khmer Rouge and other anti-Vietnamese forces in Kampuchea. In addition, the United States, which has a formal alliance with Thailand under the terms of the Southeast Asia Treaty Organization (SEATO) agreement, has provided military assistance for several years (the 1985 total was $387.5 million, with a further $95 million in military sales) and maintains as close as possible a relationship with the Thais. Ultimately, though, China is too far away to do more than engage the Vietnamese along its own border and too poor to help economically. The United States can provide considerable economic, diplomatic, and material military assistance, but it is unlikely ever to be able to do more than that, given the post-Vietnam inhibitions against any further U.S. military involvement in Asia on land. Thailand thus knows that it must face its major national problems, internal and external, on its own.

Apart from the major worry of Vietnamese incursions across the Kampuchean border, Thailand has several other low-level security concerns that could potentially assume major proportions. In the far north of the country, Thai security forces have waged a long and not entirely successful war with the opium warlords, who for decades have controlled the opium trail out of the Golden Triangle area (so-called because the borders of Thailand, Laos, and Burma converge there). In the same overall region, Thailand has faced occasional trouble from Burma's attempts to put down the never-ending efforts of the Karens and other ethnically non-Burmese groups to attain their own autonomy. The Karens, who are different from the Burmese in language, physical characteristics, and religion, are the best organized of all the groups opposing rule by Rangoon. Supplies, weapons, cash, and personnel reach the Karens principally, and sometimes solely, through Thailand, giving Burmese troops a permanent source of grievance against the Thais.

There may be a more serious problem in the traditionally impoverished hilly northeast of Thailand. Several of the provinces in this huge area that nestles into the curve of the Mekong River were aflame with a major Communist insurgency during the 1960s and early 1970s, their supplies coming mainly from the Chinese, through Laos and across the Mekong. The Chinese even provided radio broadcasts from Yunnan Province, the "Voice of the People of Thailand," which propagandized for the pro-Peking Thai Communist party masterminding the revolt. When China abandoned overt support for its ideological client groups in rebellion against their host-governments in Southeast Asia in the late 1970s, the Thai Communists in the northeast were surprisingly easily persuaded to accept a generous Thai government amnesty. Former guerrilla fighters came over to the government by the hundreds. By 1981 the insurgency, which had been able to field 20,000 armed men at its height, was essentially over.

It may not, however, be totally dead. Thai military intelligence officers have reported that infiltrators from Laos, whose Mekong border inhabitants are ethnically close to the Thais of the northeast, had been attempting to reestablish links with former guerrillas in the early 1980s. The Laotians, moreover, have a dormant territorial claim to the sixteen northeastern provinces of Thailand, a claim that the Vietnamese have intermittently supported in discussions with such third countries as France, for example. Lesser but often bitter territorial disputes have also been fought out from time to time over islands and sandbanks in the Mekong River ever since the Pathet Lao took control of Laos in 1975. In the firefights that have occasionally broken out over these issues, Thais have been killed. Should Thailand's internal situation ever prove ripe for it, or should Thai armed forces become heavily involved in repulsing a major Vietnamese attack, it would not take much for the Laotians — presumably on instructions from Hanoi — to stir up into full flame the embers of the earlier Communist revolt in the northeast.

Finally, Thailand has yet another Communist insurgency in its far south, in the border region where the ethnically Thai and religiously Buddhist culture of the Thai majority gives way to the

ethnically Malay and religiously Islamic culture of neighboring
Malaysia. Though Thailand and Malaysia, as members of ASEAN,
have good relations, tensions over Thai handling of the Islamic
minorities have often been exacerbated by open Malay sympathy
for their Thai fellow Moslems. In addition, the Thai-Malay border
region has traditionally been an area where forces of the Communist party of Malaya have operated. From Bangkok's point of
view, the troubles in its southern provinces are under control, but
they remain potential problem areas.

The challenges of domestic Communist insurgency, frictions with
neighboring Laos and Burma, and the ethnically Malay minority
dissatisfactions have been with Thailand for the better part of three
to four decades. In many respects, indeed, security considerations
have dominated the domestic national political debate in Thailand.
For several hundred years under an absolute monarchy, albeit a
generally benevolent one, Thais have historically felt comfortable
with a strong, indeed authoritarian, central government. Even after
1932, when the power of the Thai monarch was reduced from
absolute to constitutionally limited, a sense of firm authority at
the center was provided by the Thai military. Since then, all attempts to move Thailand institutionally toward a political democracy have been hampered by the determination of Thailand's military
leaders to maintain a near-veto influence over the direction of Thai
politics. Usually, the intervention of the Thai military has been
rationalized as a move to defend the throne and the political integrity of the nation. In practice, though the king has played an
important and at times vital role in Thai internal developments,
he has been as much at the mercy of recalcitrant generals as the
rest of the Thai people have been.

Experts differ on the numbers count of Thai coups and attempted
coups since the 1932 putsch that drastically modified the role of
the monarchy. By most estimates, there have been eighteen coup
attempts by the Thai military, ten of them successful. Under the
current prime minister, former army chief Prem Tinsulanond, sixty-
five, there have been two coup attempts since he was elected
premier in 1980, the most recent of them in September 1985. There

has also been at least one assassination attempt. Some Thais dismiss
the military comings and goings as nothing more than political
hiccups in an otherwise socially well-ordered political scenę. A
former senior Thai diplomat in the United States dismisses Thai
coups as "Mickey Mouse coups." He adds: "They may flash big
headlines in the *New York Times* and the *Washington Post,* or they
may get depicted on the tube in the United States in people's living
rooms, but all in all, I think that this is basically a stable, peaceful,
and moderate country."

In many respects, this observation is correct. Thailand indeed
has a fundamentally contented society that believes devoutly in
the trio of national principles: monarchy, nation, religion. Tradition has played a major role in maintaining social stability throughout the vicissitudes of national politics of the past five decades and
during the particularly stressful years of the 1960s and 1970s. In
addition, the fact that 80 percent of Thailand's population is still
rural, and that the country is one of only six nations in the world
that consistently export food, adds a formidable dimension of so-
lidity to the often volatile context of Thailand as a developing
nation.

Without coming to know Thailand well, foreigners generally do
not appreciate just how traditionally minded — and hence stable — most of Thai society is. The country might arguably be regarded as one of the best socially integrated of all East Asian Pacific
Rim societies. The qualification that needs to be made is in deter-
mining whether Thailand's endemic "coupitis," as it might be
termed, is a manageable element of the Thai polity and likely
to be cured eventually with the gradual strengthening of parliamentary institutions, or whether it reflects some social instability
concealed below the placid surface of Thai life. Even in "Mickey
Mouse coups," people get killed, economic and social life is in-
terrupted, the military is distracted from its primary task of de-
fending the country, and foreigners worry. Yet the very frequency
of Thai coups renders them less of an overall threat to the country
than they might otherwise be. Clumsy and violent as they often
are, Thai coups appear to be part of an overall political process

in a society where other norms for settling major conflicts of interest in a democratic political way have not yet caught hold. In Thailand, generals see themselves informally as sort of "electors" of Thai governments, justifying their extralegal intervention in national life as an outgrowth of a quasi-guardian role in Thai national life assumed by the Thai army ever since the emergence of constitutional monarchy in the 1930s.

For all that, there are some danger signs. One is the poverty of life in the northeast and other rural areas, for example. It has thrown huge numbers of Thai women — by some estimates as many as 100,000 — into prostitution in Bangkok, Pattaya, and other tourist areas. Bangkok itself has often been termed "the sex capital of the world," a label that may provoke sniggers of amused recognition among Western businessmen and tourists but can hardly be flattering to self-respecting Thais. In addition to the misery that results from forced prostitution, it has incalculable ripple effects of corruption and crime — not to mention disease — in the society at large. There are bar owners, pimps, and protection gangs to be reckoned with, police payoffs, and never-far-distant risk of violence whenever prostitution is rampant. In Bangkok in particular, an overcrowded city whose fundamental infrastructure is already inadequate and where corruption is rife, prostitution on its present scale ought to be seen for what it is, a social problem with a fundamentally demoralizing and destabilizing impact upon the city's, and the nation's, life.

Fortunately for the country, and to the credit of its well-trained and serious-minded managers for the past three decades, the Thai economy performed well at the same period in which other Pacific Rim economies were also riding the crest of a rapidly expanding world trade system. Thailand's economy has rested on the dual pillars of a very strong resource base and a two-decade background of rapid economic growth. That, along with an excellent location, promising offshore energy resources, and a low-cost labor force, raises considerably the country's reputation as an area of investment opportunity.

Between 1960 and 1979 the economic growth rate averaged 7

to 8 percent annually. Not only did this help offset many of the usual sources of social and political discontent in the country, it gave the Thais breathing space to restructure their economic base substantially. Agriculture diversified from mainly rice to other crops, for example, pineapples, papayas, and palm oil, for export. From about 1970 onward, the country's fledgling industry moved away from import substitution to export-oriented products such as garments, jewelry, and electronics. The expansion helped keep unemployment figures down.

Independent though Thailand was in food production, its vulnerability to outside pressures nevertheless became painfully apparent during 1979–1980, when the massive OPEC oil price increases shocked the Thai economy. Growth rates declined to the 5 to 6 percent level and threatened to float lower. Unemployment increased. Meanwhile, the overall decline in world prices for commodities other than oil greatly reduced Thailand's export earnings from lumber, rice, tin, and other raw materials. As the world's second largest producer of tungsten and the third largest of tin, Thailand was particularly affected by the precipitous drop of world tin prices during 1985. Other serious commodity price plunges affected sugar, a major Thai export, where the market average dropped to 5 cents a pound from 8.5 cents in 1983, and palm oil, whose market price fell 30 percent. In 1983, Thailand's trade deficit was $4.9 billion, a major problem in a country whose GNP in 1984 was only $36.1 billion. It had improved to an estimated $2.2 billion for 1985, but many Thai economists remained concerned. "The Thai economy," observed Dr. Snoh Unakul, general secretary of the Office of National Economic and Social Development Board, "is going through a tough and painful adjustment period."

Today, Thailand's economic situation, shaken by the commodity collapse, might be much more serious than it in fact is if farsighted management had not thought through some of the emergent problems at the beginning of the decade. Thailand is only 50 percent dependent upon foreign energy imports now, having started an extensive petroleum exploration program in the Gulf of Thailand. Inflation is at a modest 3 to 4 percent and shows no imminent sign of increasing rapidly. What concerns Thai economists are two primary problems. The first is Thailand's financial integrity and the creditworthiness of the economy as a whole, a vital ingredient in eligibility for both commercial and IMF project funding. The second is the risk of a domestic recession. The government of Prime Minister Prem last year was forced into austerity measures that included a zero-growth budget and currency devaluation. A large number of Thai firms went bankrupt. To these factors has been added the complication of an estimated 500,000 Thai youths newly joining the job market each year. For Dr. Snoh Unakul the sum of all this was that 1985, economically speaking, was "the worst year in memory, for many decades."

Snoh, like many Thais, exhibits a comforting, long-term optimism despite the grim, short-term economic forecasts. "We are still confident," he adds, "that we'll be able to weather the storm, and keep on with our long-term development objectives, provided that the OECD countries do not blow up the whole world, not just with nuclear weapons, but also with societal, economic policies of protectionism and the old beggar-thy-neighbor policies." Another prominent economist, Minister of Industry Dr. Chirayu Isarangkun Na Ayuthaya, echoes this fundamentally sanguine view of things. "Basically," he asserted in a conversation with U.S. businessmen in November 1985, "this is a good and solid country. This area, as you know, is the fastest growth area in the world, and in spite of the problems we have to face, it will remain a fast-growth area."

Many American business executives are certainly aware of this already. Thailand's huge agricultural production, coupled with continuing diversification of output, has opened up a vigorous market for imported agricultural and food-related equipment; processing and packaging machinery has also been in great demand. Since manufactured goods account for only 35 percent of all exports from Thailand, U.S. sales opportunities in supplying machinery and equipment for manufacturing industries may still be relatively limited. On the other hand, computer and office automation equipment imports have grown at a prodigious rate. Another area where the United States has a special advantage: hospital equipment, which is popular in Thailand because so many of the country's physicians had their training in the United States. Though Thailand is notorious for the slowness of its bureaucracy to act, and import tariffs can often be high, Americans have as good an opportunity as anyone else to bring their products into the Thai market.

Thailand itself needs to respond to U.S. charges that Thai industry is heavily protected from U.S. imports by tariffs and restrictions far more onerous than those the U.S. imposes upon Thailand. Some Thai economists own up to this, pointing out to their government that their nation's case against U.S. protectionism is undermined by the protectionist restrictions still existing in their own society. Even without any escalation of the protectionist sentiment in the United States, the Thai economy will need skillful handling domestically and sympathy from international lenders and its trading partners over the next few years.

The United States, meanwhile, should pay attention to the Thai security situation. Former Philippine Foreign Minister Carlos Romulo, with a certain amount of Filipino theatricality, once described Thailand as "a Wall of Freedom" in Asia. What he meant was that Thailand is the frontline state of the Association of Southeast Asian Nations (ASEAN) in the regional organization's efforts to contain the destabilizing energies of Hanoi. At a lunch for the *Time* Newstour, a senior Thai official also reminded American listeners of another, older metaphor. He said, "Not too long ago, Thailand was viewed by many as the 'next domino to fall.' 'Domino' though we might have been, we are one that need not fall. We have come a long way since the collapse of Indochina." The official described the Vietnamese occupation of Kampuchea as "a serious and direct threat to the security of Thailand. . . . Had it not been for Vietnam's expansionist ambition together with the support of its patron, the Soviet Union," he added, "the Kampuchean problem would not have existed at all."

No country on the Pacific Rim apart from China has had to be more wary of the hegemonistic impulses of Vietnam than Thailand.

Bordering for 1,590 miles the two Vietnam-dominated states of Laos and Kampuchea, Thailand has been the reluctant front-seat viewer of Vietnam's struggles from the 1940s on. As the fighting during four decades thrashed and clawed its way over the Indo-china peninsula, Thailand frequently found itself dragged into the conflict. Sometimes, for example during the 1960s, it suffered from a major Communist insurgency that seemed to parallel its neigh-bors' internal strife. The fabric of Thai society itself was being torn at from within.

More recently, during the seven long years in which Vietnam has tried to break the back of Khmer national resistance to its rule in Kampuchea, Thailand has seen the threat as an external one, the danger of an all-powerful, Vietnamese-led trio of Communist states imperiling its own long-term political independence. During 1985, Vietnamese troops repeatedly, and knowingly, crossed over into Thai territory in their most determined efforts so far to flush out the base camps of the three main anti-Vietnamese resistance movements. Each time, the Thais eventually forced them back, but not without sustaining civilian and military casualties. The Thais for the most part do not believe that Vietnam plans at any stage to mount a full-scale invasion of their country. For one thing, the Chinese would almost certainly respond with a counterinva-sion of Vietnam on their own. What the Thais do know, though, is that if Hanoi mounted a full-scale assault against them, their own army of 275,000 men could not match the might of any major part of Vietnam's army of 1.2 million.

Thus, for most senior officials in the Thai government, the po-litical fanaticism of the Pol Pot regime, which continues to horrify the world, is a much less important danger for Thailand than Vietnam's attempts to install its own puppet regime amenable to a Hanoi-based hegemony over Indochina. Vietnam's intention, a senior Thai official insists, "is that Kampuchea is integral and an unremovable part of the socialist Indochinese bloc. I feel that they think in 1990, by the strategy of irreversibility, they hope to have full control of Kampuchea under their domination."

True as this is, Thailand has elected to play a very high-stakes game in pressuring Vietnam to desist from its objectives. It provides sanctuary, moral, material, and diplomatic support, and logistical backup for the three main resistance movements — the largest of which is the Khmer Rouge — fighting the Vietnamese. In 1985, it was unable to do more than observe in dismay as Vietnamese forces in turn overran the base camps of all three movements: first, in January, that of the Khmer People's National Liberation Front, headed by former Cambodian Premier Son Sann; then that of the Khmer Rouge in February; and finally, in March, the Tatum headquarters of guerrilla fighters loyal to Prince Norodom Sihanouk, head of the anti-Vietnamese Coalition Government of Democratic Kampuchea. Total KPNLF strength at the time was about 12,000 to 18,000 men. The Khmer Rouge had an estimated 30,000 to 40,000 men under arms.

Many Thais are nervous about their government's hard-nosed approach to the Vietnamese threat, worrying that the current policy of helping the anti-Vietnamese resistance will antagonize Hanoi even more without increasing the likelihood that Kampuchea will ever be genuinely free of Vietnamese influence. Thai foreign ministry officials have sometimes privately expressed misgivings about Bangkok's reluctance to negotiate directly with the Vietnamese over the Kampuchean situation. A former Thai diplomat told a group of visiting Americans late in 1985 that he thought neither ASEAN nor Vietnam had expended enough efforts to search for a political solution.

Short of such a benign political development, Bangkok has no alternative but to continue its confrontational approach to Hanoi. Supported strongly by ASEAN, the United States, and most Western powers, Thailand has in fact succeeded in depriving the Heng Samrin government in Phnom Penh of international legitimacy by preventing its representatives from occupying the Kampuchea seat at the UN. Instead, Kampuchea is represented in New York by representatives of the Coalition Government of Democratic Kampuchea, the anti-Vietnamese Khmer resistance. ASEAN itself has been the principal vehicle for Thailand's diplomatic offensive against Vietnam, repeating at each annual meeting of the six foreign ministers the organization's condemnation of the Vietnamese occupation of Kampuchea. At the July 1985 meeting, however, the group did at least inch forward in the matter of negotiations, proposing "proximity" talks — that is, conducted through a diplomatic intermediary — between the three Kampuchean resistance factions and representatives of the Heng Samrin government. The Vietnamese rejected the proposal.

Much as they support Thailand's position vis-à-vis Vietnam, ASEAN member-states must wonder how long they can hold out in a confrontational approach toward Vietnam. Founded in 1967 at Thailand's initiative, the organization was a conscious effort to help the non-Communist countries of the region support each other without entanglements with outside powers, i.e., the United States, the Soviet Union, or China. At the very height of the Vietnam conflict, in 1971, ASEAN proposed transforming Southeast Asia into a Zone of Peace, Freedom, and Neutrality (ZOPFAN). The notion was both the expression of yearning for an end to the war in Indochina and a gentle signal to the United States that, in the long run, the ASEAN states, however pro-Western they might individually or corporately be, did not want to be mere ciphers in the endless rivalry between Washington and Moscow.

The United States supported the proposal. The Vietnamese, doubtless inspired by Moscow, did not, and countered with ZOGIFAN, a Zone of Genuine Independence, Freedom, and Neutrality. "Freedom," of course, was never welcome, and "Genuine Independence" meant a divorce from the West and warm association with the Soviet bloc. Yet even today, despite significant military assistance from the United States, ASEAN has made no serious effort to turn its six component states (Thailand, Malaysia, Singapore, Indonesia, the Philippines, Brunei) into a credible military power. Joint military exercises do take place, and the general staffs of ASEAN states visit one another. Yet ASEAN's anti-Vietnamese diplomacy, as the foreign ministries of the ASEAN states are certainly aware, is not backed by any visible efforts by the organization to be seen, even in a purely defensive mode, as a military entity. If, moreover, any ASEAN member country were to fall prey to a successful Communist insurgency, ASEAN has no evident contingency plans to cope with such a major threat to its internal cohesion as an organization.

The U.S. role in support of Thailand's opposition to Vietnam has an ambivalent air to it. In an odd reversal of roles, the Reagan administration for several months resisted the idea of any U.S. aid even to the non-Communist anti-Vietnamese groups operating out of Thailand. When, in July 1985, the Congress voted to provide at least token aid to the groups — a total of $10 million during 1986 and 1987 — the administration went along almost reluctantly. Unconfirmed reports in July in Washington alleged CIA covert support for the Khmer resistance, but such aid, if it exists, has never been acknowledged by either the alleged donors or the purported recipients.

Publicly, Washington has sought to follow ASEAN's lead in opposing Vietnam, a posture that has evidently caused some dismay in ASEAN itself. During Secretary of State Shultz's tour of Southeast Asia in July 1985, Singapore's Foreign Minister S. Dhanabalan expressed himself vigorously on this subject. He said, "We are not happy with the approach that the U.S. will just follow the ASEAN lead. We wish the U.S. would take a more active part in this problem." On hearing this remark quoted for him in Malaysia, Shultz tartly retorted that Dhanabalan had also expressed the wish that the United States not be "too independent." Pressed to explain why the United States was not supplying more assistance to keep the Vietnamese under military pressure, Shultz said that he didn't think the United States should always have to be the country to supply such military help. It would be better, he thought, to keep the program at its current level. Then he added: "Congress is a very changeable operation, and they are in favor of something at one time and then some things can happen and they can change their mind and all of a sudden you've got a program that's working that gets derailed. We'd like to avoid that. It's very disruptive to the sustainability of a program."

The sentiment is understandable, but shortsighted. Thailand's inherent cohesiveness as a society is arguably as solid as that of any of the other ASEAN states and it has a strong claim to vigorous U.S. support. It has, moreover, borne a larger share of national discomfort through its close and visible alliance over the years with the United States than any other country in Southeast Asia aside from South Vietnam, Laos, and Kampuchea. As the Thai official quoted earlier noted, "We were with you in Korea, we were with you in Vietnam. Not only were we with you, but we came down together, rather hard on our seats." The Thais, indeed, feel as strong a sense of alliance with and sympathy toward the United States as any country in the region except the Philippines. A more cogent argument for the United States to be less passive in its support for ASEAN resistance to the Vietnamese efforts to control Indochina completely is that, if Thailand should falter or suffer a major military setback at the hands of the Vietnamese, the integrity of ASEAN itself would be at stake.

For all of its problems and shortcomings, Thailand still represents a far more humane and promising social model for the rest of Southeast Asia than anything put together by the ideologues in Hanoi. Its natural resources, large population, ample food resources, and exports, along with a highly educated and talented economic leadership, give it the potential for a national development as far-reaching as that already achieved by the four NICs of Hong Kong, South Korea, Singapore, and Taiwan. Especially promising has been the development of natural gas resources along Thailand's eastern seaboard. In addition, Thailand's long history of political independence and the absence of colonial scars in the national psyche provide the country with emotional resources to resist external aggression and overcome internal challenges that some other, economically more successful, countries in the region might lack.

Individual Americans in the business community may not be able directly to influence U.S. policy toward Thailand, but they are capable, as in the case of the Philippines, of providing a climate in which a more affirmative U.S. support for the Thai government seems a natural rather than an artificial development. As in the Philippines, Americans are broadly popular in Thailand and their commercial presence is welcomed by the Thais as a counterweight to that of the ubiquitous Japanese.

Popularity aside, Americans are as well placed as the Japanese to penetrate Thai markets, and in key areas, such as offshore oil equipment, agricultural processing and packaging, and advanced business equipment, the United States is better positioned than Japan to offer what Thailand's rapidly changing market needs. American corporations may find that selling goods and services in Thailand requires a much longer-range approach to planning and marketing than in, say, Hong Kong or Taiwan, where the profit turnaround, especially in Hong Kong, is much faster.

More traditional than Taiwan, much less urbanized than Hong Kong, Thailand may require a U.S. investment and business approach closer to that successfully adopted by some large American companies in China. In the People's Republic, IBM, among other large U.S. corporations, has invested enormous capital in the development of indigenous Chinese training and technical support bases for its equipment in different parts of the country. It is gambling that the Chinese will favor an overall packaged approach to the importation of foreign technology over barebones purchasing schemes. This "infrastructural" attitude toward the development of new markets has already successfully been demonstrated, on a broad scale, by Japanese companies all over the world. There are, naturally, many differences between the Chinese and the Thai commercial environments, to put it mildly. Yet both require innovative approaches by U.S. companies intent on unearthing new business. China is already opening up. Still, Thailand may in many respects offer one of the great new business opportunity areas of the Pacific Rim.

9

CONCLUSIONS

NO REGION ON EARTH has grown so rapidly in the past two decades as the Pacific Rim. No other area has expanded its trade with the United States so rapidly. None has depended so much for its economic prosperity on the generosity of U.S. markets or for its political security on the presence in the region of U.S. power and alliances. Washington did not consciously map out a strategy for economic and political progress in East Asia after World War II, as it did so strikingly in Europe with the Marshall Plan. Yet the effects of the U.S. policy of openness in trade have been hardly less beneficial for the non-Communist community of East Asia than the Marshall Plan was for Western Europe. The Pacific Rim has produced an "economic miracle" in the 1980s in its own way as significant as that which grew out of the ruins of Western Europe in the 1950s and 1960s.

What is different about the "Asian miracle" is that it has gone so largely unnoticed. Preoccupation with the American trade deficit with Asia has blinded many people to one very obvious but very important point: the Pacific Rim as a whole is the one great world success story since World War II for the quintessentially American ideas of economic growth, business freedom, social development, and, yes, even political democracy. "These [Pacific Rim] countries," Seiji Naya, director of the East-West Center's Resource Systems Institute in Honolulu told an interviewer from the Asian *Wall Street Journal*, "are 'A' students of the United States." However different the cultural backgrounds of the Pacific Rim countries are from the United States's, their economic growth has been singularly a result of the application of free-market economics to their societies.

In some cases, notably South Korea, Singapore, and Taiwan, there has been extensive government coordination of business efforts. Yet it has been the risk-taking, energy, and skills of profit-minded individuals leading both small and major Pacific Rim corporations, not government planning and organization by bureaucrats, that has transformed the region over a two-decade period. While many Americans focused in anguish upon the Vietnam War and the failure of American political and military strategy there, most of the remainder of Southeast Asia was entering into a period of economic prosperity and political stability unparalleled in the region in modern times.

When the Pacific Rim economic surge first manifested itself clearly, not all Americans were eager to be told about it. For some, the trauma of Vietnam had rendered all thoughts about Asia inherently painful. For others, when the massive growth of trade with the United States within the Pacific Rim community was too obvious to ignore, it was seen only in negative terms, as a flood of Japanese and Southeast Asian imports and consequent threats to such traditional U.S. industries as textiles and steel. Overlooked in all the irritation with cheaper Asian wage rates and suspicions of dumping was one important, and for U.S. industry, highly promising, corollary of the Pacific Rim trade boom: the emergence of new market fields overseas for U.S. products. Overwhelmed as U.S. exports to Asia clearly were by imports from the region, in absolute terms they grew significantly. American sales to Japan more than doubled between 1975 and 1985, from $9.6 billion to $22.6 billion. Sales to Hong Kong more than tripled, from $0.8 billion to $2.8. At the same time, an enormous new field opened up in China, whose trade with the United States shot up from less than $1 billion during the early 1970s to more than $7 billion in 1985. Over this period, too, the United States had a favorable trade balance with China of several billion dollars. Worries about Pacific Rim protectionist problems are real enough (tobacco, movies, insurance, and financial services), but they ought not to obscure the far more important factor of the huge potential for U.S. trade in the area.

Also overlooked by many potential American sellers in the Asian market is the growing sophistication of product demand throughout the region. It is true that U.S. consumer products have done well in hitherto unexpected areas (Max Factor cosmetics in Japan, tobacco in Hong Kong). Yet many high-technology markets, in which U.S. goods are frequently at a competitive advantage compared with those from Japan and any other Western country, have opened up in Pacific Rim locations unlikely to have been foreseen as U.S. export destinations a decade ago. Such market areas could not have come into existence at all but for the ability of their host countries to build on their foreign exchange and overall economic infrastructure bases through consistent exports to the rich U.S. consumer market. High-technology demand in the Pacific Rim societies is almost certain to grow, to the advantage of enterprising and energetic American corporations, as the region continues to forge ahead economically.

The Pacific Rim's economic prosperity has plainly had a significant impact upon its political stability, reducing — except in the case of the Philippines, where the economy went badly wrong under Marcos — the threats of local Communist insurgency to their lowest point in decades. At the same time, the arbitrariness of autocracy in some of the non-Communist Pacific Rim countries has increasingly been challenged by the emergence of an educated middle class along with rising living standards and rising political expectations. A slow but steady political evolution has been under way in Taiwan for some years. In the Philippines, which had a pre-Marcos tradition of democracy and one of the best-educated populations in East Asia, natural — not Communist-inspired or led — pressures for an end to dictatorship surged forth to overwhelm President Marcos in early 1986. South Korea may be a much harder case, for reasons that have already been discussed in detail. The threat from the North is too real and the support by the military for President Chun too solid to suggest any close parallel with the Philippine developments in the foreseeable future. Sooner or later, though, if there is no invasion by the North, parliamentary democracy is likely to return to South Korea. It will do so when the business community as a whole is convinced that the economy will not seriously suffer through the uncertainties of transition to a new, full democratic regime, and when it seems likely that South Korea's security as a whole will not be threatened by such a change.

These sunny scenarios all depend on two things: the absence of any major increase in regional protectionism, and the lack of any serious military conflict within the region.

Protectionism would in some respects be a more tragic way of undermining the growing strength of the Pacific Rim community than war, for it is the one eventuality that could be initiated only by the Pacific Rim community itself, and in particular by the United States. A major regional war, on the other hand, is far more likely to be started by the actions of one of East Asia's Communist states.

An outburst of protectionism would prove to be a real scourge for the Pacific Rim. Punitive trade discrimination as a response to serious trade imbalance tends to be more a spreader of the disease than its cure: it has a way of multiplying itself far beyond the circle of countries against which it is originally aimed. Protectionist measures imposed by Washington against the Pacific Rim countries that have large trade surpluses with the United States could have ripple effects around the world. The retaliation from the directly affected countries would be rapid. But other effects might follow. Europe could play copycat, triggering an epidemic of counterreactions among a large section of the world's trading nations. At this point, something approaching a collapse in world trade would be in the offing.

Though the United States itself would survive, the Pacific Rim, quite simply, would be devastated by a trade war. A global protectionist plague could unravel three patient decades of nation building, economic growth, improved social welfare, and political security. With living standards, which have risen astronomically in two decades almost entirely through trade expansion, suddenly collapsing into an abyss, the political structure of most of the developing countries of the Pacific Rim could crumble. Urban and rural insurgencies, civil war, and the inevitable triumph of totalitarian regimes of the left or the right — but more probably of the left — would be likely developments under these circumstances. Probably only Japan, Australia, and New Zealand would remain relatively stable in the wake of a real world trade war, and even Japan might succumb to the authoritarian and militarist temptations of the 1930s. For the United States, the setback to its strategic position in the Pacific vis-à-vis its adversary, the Soviet Union, would be incalculable.

If massive protectionism is not a serious U.S. option in coping with the challenge of Pacific Rim trade competition, other responses are. Without doubt the principal offender in enjoying other countries' open markets while sheltering its own is Japan. France, West Germany, and Japan, in fact, are far more serious offenders in the protectionist sense than any of the Pacific Rim states discussed in detail in these pages. Though the Japanese government has made some efforts to improve conditions for importers, it still has a long way to go. Pressure by the United States should continue to be exerted on Tokyo to relax both tariff and nontariff barriers. At the same time, U.S. diplomacy could be effective in rounding up its Pacific Rim trading partners who also suffer from restrictive Japanese import tendencies and bring collective regional pressure to bear on the Japanese. For that matter, France and West Germany also need to hear from more than just America how disproportionately difficult it is for their own markets to be penetrated by foreign imports.

As a corollary to such steps, the United States needs to do more than it has to spread the message of free trade and economic liberty to the rest of the world. Marxism has been the great philosophical and economic failure of the century as a model for capital formation and the raising of living standards. Wherever it has been the reigning new religion, political and cultural freedoms have also suffered lamentably. There is no more powerful a demonstration of this fundamental observation about differing world views than in the Pacific Rim. Vietnam and Thailand, North and South Korea, China and Taiwan: the comparisons are embarrassing for doctrinaire socialists. The reason the United States should underline this point around the world more vigorously than it has is not to score a mere debating point with the Soviet Union. Many countries in the world that may now be wavering in their earlier commitment to socialist planning are looking to the United States for a clear reaffirmation of the underlying principles of human behavior that explain the superiority of free market economics to total state control. Ideas and theories may seem "silly," so much hot air, to commonsense Americans, but in much of the world they guide conscious behavior to a formidable degree. The Soviet Union has always understood this. Perhaps Washington should, too.

There has been a reluctance on the part of the United States to broadcast — figuratively and literally — the truth of these observations more broadly to the world. One explanation is that most Americans are not comfortable with "propaganda" even if it happens to be true. Many also tend to believe — mistakenly — that because they themselves are not interested in social and economic ideals in the abstract, the people of other countries may feel equally uneasy being confronted with them. A third point is that educated Americans, particularly career bureaucrats, often do not feel at ease expressing strong economic convictions to large audiences.

To illustrate, there is a self-consciousness about the large issues of economics and politics among many U.S. Foreign Service officers, a mistaken conviction that the vigorous endorsement of free market economics over socialist economics might amount to identifying with "Reaganism" or "right-wing" views. In fact, there is hardly any dispute at all across the liberal-conservative axis in the United States that economies broadly favoring free market processes are more efficient creators and distributors of wealth than economies dominated by centralized state planning. It is only on issues of the relative importance of government welfare programs, state intervention, and the tax/revenue debate that differences between liberals and conservatives sometimes become sharp. The United States Information Agency could greatly benefit U.S. interests around the world in general by, for example, inviting U.S. business executives from upper and middle management on short-term tours to explain to foreign audiences exactly why and how free enterprise creates and distributes wealth better than state socialism does. The equally obvious truth that there can be no political freedom without economic freedom (the reverse is not necessarily true) should also be much more broadly explained by the Voice of America and other U.S. government agencies than has hitherto been the case.

One vital aspect of the advantages that free market economies hold over state-controlled economies is the proven potential for political change. Free market economies may well thrive in strongly authoritarian countries, as South Korea and Taiwan clearly demonstrate on the Pacific Rim. But they tend to generate pluralistic forces that create the demand for a marketplace of politics to parallel the marketplace of commerce. No free market society, including South Korea and Taiwan, has been able to resist this pressure indefinitely, though governments here and there have held out for as long as they could. Taiwan, though still far from truly democratic in the Western sense, has become measurably freer in the past decade. Even South Korea has been forced by both internal and external pressures to commit itself to return to electoral politics at a specific date in the future. As for the Philippines, in early 1986 the country triumphantly demonstrated that, however corrupt and repressive an authoritarian regime may be, as long as there are still key areas of society (the church, the business community) outside of direct state control, the transformation from dictatorship to democracy can be achieved. Lamentably, not a single Marxist-ruled society has ever duplicated this transformation, a powerful argument for sustaining the distinction between authoritarian and totalitarian regimes.

The "Yellow Revolution," or "People Power," as it is alternatively called, in the Philippines also demonstrates another point that applies as much to Pacific Rim countries as to the rest of the world: the private beliefs of individuals greatly affect the capacity of the state to enforce its will. If ordinary Filipino soldiers had not believed that driving tanks over civilians — especially priests and nuns of their own Christian religion — was murder, pure and simple, and thus a higher ethical principle than obedience to military orders, Mrs. Aquino would never have become president of the Philippines. How soldiers react in the future to possibly similar orders in, say, South Korea or Taiwan will undoubtedly have a major impact upon those countries and the Pacific Rim as a region. Bearing in mind the fact that half the South Korean army is Christian (mostly Protestant), this issue is thus certainly not just academic. The U.S. administration should probably move cautiously, though, in attempting to duplicate the Philippine evolution in South Korea or Taiwan. In sobering contrast with the Philippines and, say, Spain, where democracies did arise from the ashes of burnt-out dictatorships, there are the sad cases of Nicaragua and Iran, when cruel autocracies were overthrown, only to be replaced by even crueler regimes.

The miraculous-seeming change of government in the Philippines demonstrated, yet again, the fragility of much of the politics of the Pacific Rim. In a less positive way, so did an abortive military coup in Thailand and student demonstrations in South Korea. In the context of the traumatic collapse of Indochina in the 1970s, the current political stability of East Asia is encouraging to behold. But it is not to be taken for granted. It has depended in very large measure on the emergence of China as a force for political stability in Southeast Asia and a deterrent to the ambitions of Vietnam. It has also depended on the evident resurgence of the American political will to maintain a strong presence in the Pacific Rim despite the debacle of the Vietnam War. The Chinese invasion of Vietnam in 1979, however costly in military terms, provided a powerful psychological boost to neighboring countries hitherto mesmerized by the seeming invincibility and invulnerability of the Vietnamese state. No less important have been the clear evidences of U.S. political intent in East Asia: the close U.S. alliance with

Japan, the unmistakable American commitment to South Korea, and the continuing U.S. encouragement of ASEAN's growing maturity.

The powerful U.S. presence in East Asia has been as effective as, in a sense, it has been unnoticed by most Americans. Like a clearly marked burglar alarm, it has its effect by being seen and being known to work. Most Americans are unaware that G.I.'s who patrol the Joint Security Area at Panmunjom between North and South Korea are, in a measure, human burglar alarms. The fact that, if Pyongyang planned an invasion of the South, Americans would have to be killed in the first seconds of hostilities helps keep South Korea safe. Discomforting as this fact is, it has provided South Korea with the margin of military security needed to move forward in its impressive economic growth. It has also, ironically, provided China with evidence of the continuing seriousness of the American commitment to overall security in East Asia.

Other areas where either military hostilities or the potential for them still exists are in Indochina and — though at a far lower level — across the Taiwan Straits. Thailand has continued to suffer from the depredations of Vietnamese troops attempting to wipe out resistance to their total control of Kampuchea. The probability of an outbreak of general Vietnamese-Thai hostilities is certainly not high, but it cannot be totally ruled out. A continuation of firm and high-level U.S. support for Thailand is thus essential in order to convey no signals to Hanoi that Washington is less committed to a free and independent Thailand than before.

In the China-Taiwan equation, the United States is in a delicate position. It is very important not to offend China, whose feelings about Taiwan are extremely intense and genuine, even if they ought objectively to be weighed against the equally strong feelings of most people on Taiwan. At the same time, the United States should do everything possible to discourage Peking's sense of righteousness about Taiwan from evolving into a policy of reunification-at-all-costs. So far, the People's Republic has been true to its commitment to be "patient" about resolving the issue. As we observed, though, from time to time there are worrying indications of

Peking's latent lack of belief in the possibility that most Taiwanese may simply *never* want reunification with the People's Republic as long as the Communist party there still wields unchallenged power. Washington does not really need to "do" anything about Taiwan. But it should be especially careful not to "undo" Taiwan's own self-confidence by preventing Taipei, or discouraging it, from acquiring the essential military equipment for self-defense.

Finally, there is the Soviet Union. As many have observed, military strength is one of the few general areas of national activity in which the Soviet Union has generally excelled. In the Pacific Rim, the almost complete exclusion of Moscow from the corridors of diplomatic influence has paralleled the unequivocal commitment of most of the region to free market economics. Typically, only in Indochina, where war still wages and Communist parties rule, has the Soviet profile been high. But the profile has been a military one, and a growing one at that. Though Cam Ranh Bay and Da Nang in themselves are no match for the American presence at Clark and Subic Bay, they symbolize a Soviet commitment to become more and more influential regionally. Barely more than a decade ago, Moscow had no airfield for its planes and no safe port for its ships between Vladivostok and the island of Socotra. Now, on the coast of Indochina it has the largest forward military bases outside of the Warsaw Pact nations.

So far, Moscow's presence has been more of a potential than an actual threat. It is what the presence represents politically more than what it amounts to militarily that should concern Americans greatly in their long-term appraisal of the Pacific Rim. The issue, put succinctly, is global political will. To sustain a military presence requires energy and effort at a consistent pace over a sometimes extended period of time. Though the Soviets have suffered setbacks to their world influence before (in Egypt in 1970, for example), the predominant tendency of their actions has been for increased political influence to follow on the heels of increased military presence. In Indochina itself, this tendency has been apparent since the total eclipse of pro-Chinese elements in the Hanoi politburo since the late 1970s. In the Caribbean and Central America, the

Soviet military presence in Cuba made possible the Cuban (and thus, indirectly, Soviet) political influence in Central America (Nicaragua), and also in Southern Africa (Angola and Mozambique).

In a way that most Americans do not fully grasp, Moscow uses military presence as a form of political power. Bombers do not actually have to take off, tanks do not actually have to fire, and even crude, direct threats do not have to be made. Yet the *power* is felt. And it influences events in neighboring countries. If the United States did not continue to be powerfully and visibly present in East Asia, particularly at Clark and Subic Bay, but also in South Korea, the psychological pressures that could then be exerted on the countries of the region by Moscow might well be too powerful to resist. The currently non-Communist governments of the region would not even have to be overthrown by Communist insurgency or destroyed by civil war or foreign invasion. From Moscow's point of view it would simply be enough if they were unequivocally aware of who the new regional power was, what its priority interests were, and thus how not to offend it diplomatically. In that equation, without a shot being fired, the direction of the evolution of the Pacific Rim could be changed decisively, and with it the course of the world's history.

The Soviet presence is clearly a challenge to the United States in the Pacific Rim, a challenge that can be met and overcome by steady nerves, clear vision, and a continuing commitment. But from a nonmilitary point of view, with or without the Soviet Union, the region offers exhilarating openings for a different kind of American presence. In many respects, the growth and changes rushing forward in the Pacific Rim today offer the greatest opportunities for U.S. business to expand its export earnings in two or three decades. These opportunities have been greatly enhanced in the short term by the rise in the value of the Japanese yen against the dollar, a development that moves many U.S. goods into strong competitive positions in Japan and other Pacific Rim countries.

There is nothing supernatural about Japanese production and trading skills, however skillfully the Japanese have come to dominate the markets of East and Southeast Asia. Japanese management techniques have been well studied and certain clear strengths in the entire Japanese social structure of industry have been identified. The "vertical," i.e., company-oriented, structure of Japanese labor unions and the paternalistic nature of Japanese big business employment practices are among factors identified as providing much higher levels of company loyalty, and hence productivity, than those in the United States. The Japanese have also consistently pioneered in the use of industrial robots for manufacturing purposes. More than half of all the industrial robots in the world are in Japan, a fact that must say something to U.S. manufacturers about the value of automation.

Against Japanese corporate enthusiasm, the United States has at least the offsetting value of greater corporate flexibility. The hiring and firing practices of American companies often horrify the Japanese, but in many cases they result in the best available talent arriving in the best U.S. corporations at the right time. Nowhere, though, is the structure of U.S. industry at a greater advantage vis-à-vis Japan and any other Pacific Rim country than in the high-technology field. Rapid innovations in computer software, swift company start-ups, and research and development initiatives have enabled American computer firms to establish a firm foothold in both Japan and most of the Pacific Rim. In addition, the American lead in aerospace shows no sign of being seriously challenged in the Pacific Rim. Finally, Americans, though they are not Asian, have distinct advantages in selling their products in the Pacific Rim. They are generally liked, and they are still regarded from the World War II era very largely as liberators. In the business field alone, the Pacific Rim is perhaps the most exciting new field of opportunity that America will have in front of it in the twenty-first century.

Where the United States has a lot of catching up to do in selling its wares in the Pacific is in the basic infrastructure of marketing. There is still far too little fundamental familiarity with language, society, and market among many American companies interested in breaking into the Asian field. Not enough Americans know the area's languages, and not enough corporations have grasped the tremendous value, over the long term, of intimacy with the social and economic needs of a given society. A consistent explanation of Japanese marketing success in the Pacific Rim, as well as in the rest of the world, is the thoroughness with which Japanese companies tend to study a given area before making any major marketing decision in it. A mutually beneficial relationship between U.S. business and the U.S. academic community could evolve if American business funded more college Asian area study programs that could turn out Asian-oriented business or economics majors. Many U.S. corporations might also find that the kind of mind that can master the intricacies of Asian languages and cultures can also make intelligent and subtle business decisions based on analysis of complex and diverse data. Asian studies graduates, in short, might be doubly useful to large and small U.S. corporations looking toward the Pacific Rim.

As a region and a concept, the Pacific Rim is in the world to stay. Americans should be ready to plunge into it. President Theodore Roosevelt certainly understood this. Surveying prophetically at the turn of this century the Pacific and its vital future importance to the world, he saw clearly how decisive the United States should be in participating in the affairs of the region. "We do not have a choice," he said, "as to whether we will or will not play a great part in this area, we must play a great part." From such a "great part" great blessings for the United States are likely to flow. To Roosevelt's words, therefore, let Americans say Amen.